CHILDREN'S ISSUES, LAWS AND PROGRAMS

THE CHILD ABUSE PREVENTION AND TREATMENT ACT WITH A SUMMARY OF STATE LAWS

CHILDREN'S ISSUES, LAWS AND PROGRAMS

Additional books in this series can be found on Nova's website under the Series tab.

Additional E-books in this series can be found on Nova's website under the E-book tab.

SOCIAL ISSUES, JUSTICE AND STATUS

Additional books in this series can be found on Nova's website under the Series tab.

Additional E-books in this series can be found on Nova's website under the E-book tab.

CHILDREN'S ISSUES, LAWS AND PROGRAMS

THE CHILD ABUSE PREVENTION AND TREATMENT ACT WITH A SUMMARY OF STATE LAWS

CRAIG S. FIKET
AND
AMY W. GROTTI
EDITORS

Nova Science Publishers, Inc.
New York

For permission to use material from this book please contact us:
Telephone 631-231-7269; Fax 631-231-8175
Web Site: http://www.novapublishers.com

Library of Congress Cataloging-in-Publication Data

The Child Abuse Prevention and Treatment Act with a summary of state laws / editors, Craig S. Fiket and Amy W. Grotti.
p. cm.
Includes index.
ISBN 978-1-62100-051-8 (hardcover)
1. Child abuse--Law and legislation--United States. 2. Child abuse--Law and legislation--United States--States. 3. United States. Child Abuse Prevention and Treatment Act. I. Fiket, Craig S. II. Grotti, Amy W. III. Stoltzfus, Emilie. IV. Child Welfare Information Gateway (U.S.)
KF9323.C563 2011
344.7303'276--dc23

2011030095

Published by Nova Science Publishers, Inc. † New York

CONTENTS

PREFACE

This book discusses the issues and scope of child abuse and neglect; the response of the CPS agencies, the identified risk factors for poor child and family outcomes among all children in families investigated for abuse or neglect, as well as a detailed description of the current programs and activities authorized under the Child Abuse Prevention and Treatment Act (CAPTA) and their funding.

Chapter 1- Child abuse and neglect is a significant social concern. Children who experience abuse and/or neglect are more likely to have developmental delays and impaired language or cognitive skills; be identified as "problem" children (with attention difficulties or challenging behaviors); be arrested for delinquency, adult criminality, and violent criminal behavior; experience depression, anxiety, or other mental health problems as adults; engage in more health-risk behaviors as adults; and have poorer health outcomes as adults. Further, data from a nationally representative sample of children in families investigated for abuse or neglect show that as a whole—and without regard to whether a child protective services (CPS) investigator determines that abuse or neglect has occurred—children in families who come into contact with CPS agencies are at higher risk for poor development and behavior outcomes than children in the general population. In addition, that survey shows that these children live in families that often face challenges to their ability to care for and nurture their children, including trouble paying for basic necessities, low social support, and only one supportive caregiver in the family. In FY2007, states reported an estimated 3.5 million children were in families investigated or assessed by CPS workers and some 794,000 were identified as victims of abuse or neglect.

Chapter 2- Child abuse and neglect are defined by Federal and State laws. The Federal Child Abuse Prevention and Treatment Act (CAPTA) provides minimum standards that States must incorporate in their statutory definitions of child abuse and neglect. The CAPTA definition of "child abuse and neglect," at a minimum, refers to:

- "Any recent act or failure to act on the part of a parent or caretaker, which results in death, serious physical or emotional harm, sexual abuse, or exploitation, or an act or failure to act which presents an imminent risk of serious harm"

In: The Child Abuse Prevention and Treatment ... ISBN: 978-1-62100-051-8
Editors: Craig S. Fiket, Amy W. Grotti © 2012 Nova Science Publishers, Inc.

Chapter 1

THE CHILD ABUSE PREVENTION AND TREATMENT ACT (CAPTA): BACKGROUND, PROGRAMS AND FUNDING*

Emilie Stoltzfus

SUMMARY

Child abuse and neglect is a significant social concern. Children who experience abuse and/or neglect are more likely to have developmental delays and impaired language or cognitive skills; be identified as "problem" children (with attention difficulties or challenging behaviors); be arrested for delinquency, adult criminality, and violent criminal behavior; experience depression, anxiety, or other mental health problems as adults; engage in more health-risk behaviors as adults; and have poorer health outcomes as adults. Further, data from a nationally representative sample of children in families investigated for abuse or neglect show that as a whole—and without regard to whether a child protective services (CPS) investigator determines that abuse or neglect has occurred—children in families who come into contact with CPS agencies are at higher risk for poor development and behavior outcomes than children in the general population. In addition, that survey shows that these

* This is an edited, reformatted and augmented version of Congressional Research Service Report R40899, dated November 4, 2009.

children live in families that often face challenges to their ability to care for and nurture their children, including trouble paying for basic necessities, low social support, and only one supportive caregiver in the family. In FY2007, states reported an estimated 3.5 million children were in families investigated or assessed by CPS workers and some 794,000 were identified as victims of abuse or neglect.

In 1974, Congress enacted the Child Abuse Prevention and Treatment Act (CAPTA, P.L. 93-247) to create a single federal focus for preventing and responding to child abuse and neglect. As a condition of receiving state grant funds under that act, states are required to have procedures in place for receiving and responding to allegations of abuse or neglect and for ensuring children's safety. Further, they must define child abuse and neglect in a way that is consistent with CAPTA, which defines the term as " at a minimum, any recent act or failure to act on the part of a parent or caretaker, which results in death, serious physical or emotional harm, sexual abuse or exploitation, or an act or failure to act which presents an imminent risk of serious harm."

Since its enactment, CAPTA has been reauthorized numerous times, most recently by the Keeping Children and Families Safe Act of 2003 (P.L. 108-36). Currently, it authorizes formula grants to states to help improve their child protective services; competitive grants and contracts for research, demonstration, and other activities related to better identifying, preventing, and treating child abuse and neglect; and formula grants to states for support of community-based child abuse and neglect prevention services. Funding authorization for these CAPTA programs expired with FY2008. However, Congress appropriated $110 million for CAPTA in FY2009 (P.L. 111-8) and a similar amount has been proposed for FY2010 (H.R. 3293). In addition, CAPTA authorizes grants to improve the prosecution and handling of child abuse and neglect cases. These formula grants to states, commonly referred to as Children's Justice Act grants, are funded via an annual set-aside of up to $20 million from the Crime Victims fund.

This report begins with discussion of the issue and scope of child abuse and neglect, followed by a discussion of the manner and scope of the work of the CPS agency in receiving and responding to allegations of child abuse or neglect, and then looks at some identified risk factors for poor child and family outcomes among all children in families investigated for abuse or neglect. Finally, it provides a detailed description of the current programs and activities authorized under CAPTA and discusses funding authorized and provided under CAPTA.

OVERVIEW

Child abuse and neglect is a significant social concern. Children who experience abuse or neglect are more likely to have developmental delays and impaired language or cognitive skills; be identified as "problem" children (with attention difficulties or challenging behaviors); be arrested for delinquency, adult criminality, and violent criminal behavior; experience depression, anxiety, or other mental health problems as adults; engage in more health-risk behaviors as adults; and have poorer health outcomes as adults.[1]

Between 1963 and 1967, every state and the District of Columbia enacted some form of child abuse and neglect reporting law to permit individuals to refer cases of suspected child abuse or neglect to a public agency. The rapid adoption of these laws was aided by a model reporting law disseminated by the Children's Bureau, which is housed within the Administration for Children and Families (ACF) at the U.S. Department of Health and Human Services (HHS). In 1974, Congress passed the Child Abuse Prevention and Treatment Act (CAPTA, P.L. 93-247) and state reporting laws were modified to conform to the standards it established. In creating CAPTA, Congress sought to increase understanding of child abuse and neglect and improve the response to its occurrence by establishing a single federal focal point on the issue. Since its enactment 35 years ago, the law has been reauthorized and amended numerous times, most recently by the Keeping Children and Families Safe Act of 2003 (P.L. 108-36).[2] Currently, CAPTA authorizes:

- ***State Grants***: Formula grants to states and territories to help improve their child protective service (CPS) systems, in exchange for which states must comply with various requirements related to the reporting, investigation, and treatment of child maltreatment cases. The FY2009 appropriation was $26.5 million.
- ***Discretionary Activities***: Federal data collection, dissemination, and technical assistance efforts related to child abuse prevention and treatment, as well as competitive grants to a range of eligible entities for research and demonstration projects or other activities related to the identification, prevention, and treatment of child abuse or neglect. The FY2009 appropriation was $41.8 million (including a $13.5 million set-aside for the ACF home visitation initiative, $500,000 for a feasibility study related to a national child abuse and neglect offender registry, and $2.4 million for other congressional projects

designated in the Explanatory Statement accompanying the FY2009 appropriations bill).

- ***Community-Based Grants:*** Formula grants to each state and territory for support of community-based activities and services to prevent child abuse and neglect. The FY2009 appropriation was $41.7 million.
- ***Children's Justice Act Grants:*** Formula grants to states and territories to improve investigation, prosecution, and handling of child maltreatment cases, particularly those cases related to child sexual abuse or exploitation. For FY2009, $20 million was provided out of the federal Crime Victims Fund, including a $3 million set-aside for tribes.

Funding authorization for most grants or activities authorized under CAPTA expired with FY2008. However, as shown above, the Omnibus Appropriations Act, 2009 (P.L. 111-8) provided roughly $110 million out of the general treasury for CAPTA grants and activities in FY2009. In addition, as required by the Victims of Crime Act (P.L. 93-247, as amended), $20 million was set aside from the Crime Victims Fund for grants to improve the investigation, prosecution, and handling of child abuse and neglect cases (commonly referred to as "Children's Justice Act grants"). FY2010 appropriations legislation (H.R. 3293) pending in Congress would provide roughly the same CAPTA funding for FY2010 and, again, an additional $20 million is expected to be available from the Crime Victims Fund.

Issue and Scope

Children depend on adults to meet their physical needs, foster their social and emotional development, and, in so doing, nurture their growth into adulthood. For most children, their parents are both capable and committed to providing this necessary care and support. For some, however, this is not true. Any person who knows or suspects that a child is being abused or neglected may contact child protective services (CPS) with this information. Local CPS agencies are called on to screen these referrals, investigate or assess the allegations as warranted, and identify children in need of additional services. In carrying out this job, CPS workers must discern the difference between children whose home situations are safe, those whose homes may be made safe if additional supports and services are provided, and those for whom removal—even if temporary—is necessary for the children's protection.

This first part of this report includes a discussion of definitions of child abuse and neglect and a description of how CPS agencies receive and respond to allegations of child abuse and neglect. Tasks done by CPS workers are described, including the manner in which children are ultimately counted as "victims" or "non-victims" of child abuse or neglect. It continues with a look at certain demographic characteristics of children found to be victims and a brief description of services provided to children and their families following a child abuse or neglect investigation. Finally, this part of the report concludes with a short review of some risk factors for poor child outcomes that are seen disproportionately in children whose families are investigated for abuse or neglect, and lists some circumstances prevalent among the families or caregivers of these children that may also put these children at risk for poor outcomes.

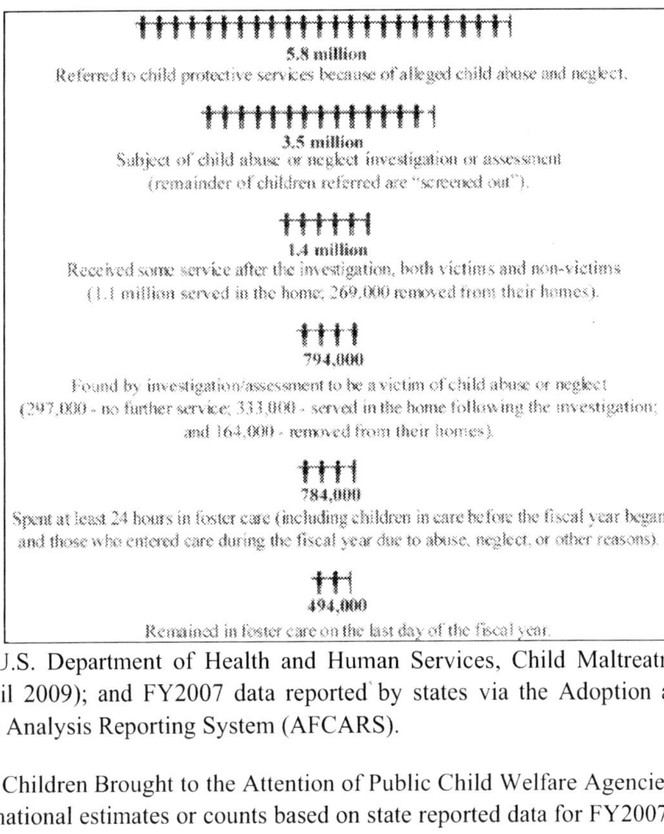

Source: U.S. Department of Health and Human Services, Child Maltreatment 2007 (April 2009); and FY2007 data reported by states via the Adoption and Foster Care Analysis Reporting System (AFCARS).

Figure 1. Children Brought to the Attention of Public Child Welfare Agencies Reflects national estimates or counts based on state reported data for FY2007.

CPS agencies are sometimes referred to as the "front-end" of the child welfare services continuum. The number of children and families who come to the attention of CPS each year is far greater than the number of children found to be victims of child abuse or neglect and the even smaller number of children who are placed in foster care. Figure 1 shows the scope of children and families who come in contact with the CPS/child welfare agency.

Definition of Child Abuse and Neglect

Child abuse and neglect is defined in CAPTA as "at a minimum, any recent act or failure to act on the part of a parent or caretaker, which results in death, serious physical or emotional harm, sexual abuse or exploitation, or an act or failure to act which presents an imminent risk of serious harm."[3] States that receive state grant funds under CAPTA must define "child abuse and neglect" to be consistent with this federal definition. All states receive CAPTA state grant funds and many states have developed more detailed definitions of child abuse and neglect, which is sometimes referred to as child maltreatment.[4] Typically, these definitions elaborate on the meaning of different types of maltreatment, including 1) physical abuse, generally involving non-accidental physical injury to the child and, in some states, substantial threat of injury; 2) neglect, including failure to provide necessary food, clothing, shelter, medical care, or supervision and, typically, for reasons other than economic inability to do so; 3) sexual abuse/exploitation; and 4) emotional abuse or mental injury. Some states also incorporate specific language defining other forms of abuse and neglect, including, for example, abandonment, or harming or exposing a child to harm because of substance abuse or the manufacture of a controlled substance.[5] Consistent with the federal definition in CAPTA, many state child abuse and neglect definitions also specify that a finding of child abuse or neglect may only occur if the perpetrator of the maltreatment is a parent or caregiver of the child.[6] In FY2007, 80% of the perpetrators in substantiated abuse or neglect cases were one or both of the child's parents, 5% were other relatives of the child, and 3% were the unmarried partner of the parent. Other types of non-parent caregivers (e.g., foster parents, residential facility staff, and legal guardians) typically represented less than one-half of 1%, each, of the perpetrators of child abuse or neglect.[7]

Receiving and Screening Allegations of Child Abuse and Neglect

States are required under the CAPTA state grant program to have a statewide law or program in effect that includes procedures for receiving and screening referrals of known or suspected child abuse and neglect, and procedures for investigating them as appropriate. In FY2007, child protective services agencies received 3.2 million allegations of abuse or neglect concerning an estimated 5.8 million children. More than one-third of the allegations (38%) were "screened out" and no investigation followed. However, investigations or assessments were conducted with regard to the majority of allegations received (62%), involving some 3.5 million children. Of these children, an estimated 794,000 were determined to be victims of child abuse or neglect—or roughly 11 children per 1,000 children in the population.[8] (For data on the number of referrals, investigations, and victims of child abuse by state, see Appendix A.)

Any person can make a child abuse and neglect allegation to CPS. Most states require certain individuals (e.g., health personnel, teachers, police officers, lawyers, and workers at social service agencies) to report any instance of known or suspected child abuse or neglect.[9] Individuals may make reports of abuse or neglect to local law enforcement or a local CPS agency, and states typically operate a 24-hour hotline to receive this information as well. Under the CAPTA state grant program, states must have procedures for cross-agency cooperation and states have policies (often in statute) regarding how information is to be shared across these entities.[10] States or localities also develop their own rules for when an allegation of child abuse or neglect will be "screened out." For example, these might include—when the allegation received does not meet the state's definition of child abuse or neglect or does not include enough information to permit an investigation or assessment to occur; when the children in the referral were determined to be the responsibility of another agency or jurisdiction (e.g., a military installation or a tribe); or when the alleged victim was older than 18. If an allegation is screened out, there is generally no additional CPS response, although, in a limited number of localities, information on screened-out allegations may be referred to community-based groups for possible follow-up.[11] By contrast, when an allegation is "screened-in," it is called a "report" and a CPS investigation or assessment follows.

Among the child abuse and neglect referrals screened in for investigation or assessment in FY2007, 58% were made by professionals—that is, individuals who encountered the alleged child victim as part of their job.

These professionals, who, as noted earlier, may be required under state law to report known or suspected abuse or neglect, included education personnel, who were the source of 17% of all reports investigated; legal, law enforcement, or criminal justice personnel (16%); social services personnel (10%); medical personnel (8%); mental health personnel (4%); and foster care or child day care providers (2%). Reports made by non-professionals in FY2007 included those made by anonymous individuals (8% of all reports investigated), relatives (7%), parent(s) (6%), and friends or neighbors of the child (5%).[12]

What Is an Investigation?

Typically, a single investigation involves more than one child. The number and rate of children who are the subject of a child abuse and neglect investigation trended upward between 1990 and 2004, but has remained relatively flat since that year. Annually, about 3.5 million to 3.6 million children are the subject of CPS investigations or assessments; this translates to a rate of roughly 48 children being the subject of an investigation (or assessment) for every 1,000 in the population.

The primary focus of an investigation is a determination concerning the safety of a child. The CPS investigator must assess risk to the child in the home—both whether abuse or neglect has already happened and whether it might occur. In addition to this task, a 2005-2006 national survey of local CPS agencies found that nearly every agency required investigators to make a separate determination of whether any other children in the family were maltreated (98%). A very large majority of these agencies (92%) also required the investigator to make an assessment of service needs of the child during the investigation and, separately, to make a recommendation for court intervention if needed. Finally, in roughly three-fourths of the local CPS agencies surveyed, investigators were required to provide short-term services to the family as necessary (during the investigation) and to refer the family for further (post-investigation) services if needed.

In making these determinations and assessments, local CPS agencies commonly instruct investigators to review any prior CPS records relevant to the family; visit the family without making an appointment; discuss the case with other CPS workers; and interview relevant individuals, such as family members other than the caregiver, professionals known to the family, witnesses, and/or the person who made the report of abuse or neglect. Other investigation activities might include conducting a criminal background check on the alleged perpetrator, conducting family group conference meetings, and discussing the case with a multi-disciplinary team.[13]

What is Alternative Response?

Some states (or localities) have implemented a system of "alternative" or "differential" response. In these places, reports of abuse or neglect where children are deemed (at the screening stage) *not* at imminent risk of harm or at lower risk may be referred for alternative response rather than investigation. An alternative response focuses primarily on assessing family strengths and needs to ensure children's safety. In many localities, referral to an alternative response precludes a formal determination that abuse or neglect occurred (or didn't occur).[14]

A 2005-2006 survey of local CPS agencies found that 39% had implemented some form of "alternative" or "differential" response.[15] That survey found that in the large majority of those agencies, workers providing an alternative response were required to follow standard practices. These included making assessments of the underlying causes of the alleged maltreatment (a standard practice at 84% of the surveyed agencies), the service needs of the family (86%), and the service needs of the child(ren) (86%). Most local CPS agencies (71%) also required the worker providing an alternative response to refer the family for further services if needed. Activities conducted as part of alternative response typically included interviews with caregiver(s) of the child(ren); interviews with (or formal observation of) the child(ren); and discussion of the case with other CPS workers. They might also include a visit to the family by appointment.[16]

Who Is Counted as a Victim?

In FY2007, HHS estimates that 794,000 children experienced child abuse or neglect, based on reports from state CPS agencies. The annual number of children reported as victims of child abuse and neglect by HHS includes all children for whom a CPS investigator "substantiates" that abuse or neglect occurred, as well as children for whom the investigator determines that the abuse or neglect is "indicated" and those coded by states as an "alternative response victim." All states report on substantiated victims of child abuse and neglect and the very large majority of children who are counted as victims (close to 96% in FY2007) had an investigation finding of "substantiated." A few states (four in FY2007) also report the number of children for whom abuse or neglect was "indicated." In these states, a CPS investigator who suspects that the child may have been maltreated (or is at risk of maltreatment) but is unable to substantiate this under the rules of evidence (see below) or the definition of abuse or neglect in the state may determine that child maltreatment is "indicated." For FY2007, four states reported that 15,000 children had an investigation determination of "indicated." Finally, although provision of alternative response typically precludes an abuse or neglect finding, two states reported in FY2007 that 16,000 children were "alternative response victims."[17]

Level of Evidence Required to Substantiate a Child Maltreatment Report

In determining whether to "substantiate" a child abuse or neglect report, a CPS investigator must consider how child abuse and neglect is defined in the state, as well as the level of evidence required by the state to make such a determination.[18] In FY2007, 20 states required investigators to make a "reasonable" determination or to have credible evidence that a child had been abused or neglected before formally substantiating a child abuse or neglect report; more states (27) used a somewhat stricter level of evidence, requiring investigators to find that a "preponderance" of evidence supported a determination that a child was a victim of abuse or neglect; and two states required the most rigorous standard of "clear or convincing evidence."[19] States with the least restrictive level of evidence had an average child maltreatment victim rate of more than 13 in FY2007, those using a somewhat more strict level of evidence had a victim rate of just below 10, and those with the most restrictive level of evidence had a victim rate just below 2.[20]

Who Is Counted as a Non-Victim?

Among all children who were the subject of a child abuse and neglect investigation in FY2007, HHS estimates that about 2.7 million were "non-victims." Children are counted as "non-victims" if they are the subject of a CPS investigation and the investigation does not conclude that they were a substantiated, indicated, or alternative response victim of abuse or neglect. For most "non-victims" (72% in FY2007), this means the CPS investigation concluded with a determination that abuse or neglect was "unsubstantiated."[21]

This finding category is used by all states but is often not defined. It is commonly understood to mean that there was not sufficient evidence under state law to conclude that the child was maltreated or was at risk of maltreatment. There is a growing body of evidence suggesting that the difference between children for whom an abuse or neglect case is substantiated as opposed to unsubstantiated may be more a matter of degree than absolute difference. As noted above, states that require stronger levels of evidence tend to have lower rates of substantiation. Further, as discussed later, children in families who are investigated for abuse or neglect, in general, exhibit greater developmental and other risk factors than do children in the general population, and many children who are not found to be victims of abuse or neglect receive post-investigation services nonetheless.

There are a variety of additional "non-victim" finding categories reported by states. More than 1 in 10 "non-victims" (13% in FY2007) had a finding of "no alleged maltreatment." This may be the result of an increasing number of states in which all children living in the home of a child for whom an abuse or neglect case is reported are viewed as subjects of the investigation. Thus, this group of non-victims is presumed to be siblings of children for whom abuse or neglect was investigated and for whom a victim determination was not made. A smaller percentage of "non-victims" (less than 8% in FY2007) are reported as having been served by an "alternative response" and with no finding of child maltreatment. (Only 11 states reported data in this category in FY2007.) "Non-victims" also include children for whom the case was "closed with no finding." In FY2007, 23 states reported "non-victims" in this category, and they represented less than 2% of "non-victims." Generally, "closed with no finding" means that the agency could not complete the investigation (e.g., because the family could not be located). Finally, in a very small number of instances (less than one-half of 1% of children subject to an investigation), the allegations of abuse or neglect are found to be "intentionally false" by the CPS investigator.[22]

Children Found to Be Victims of Abuse or Neglect

The number and rate of children who were found to be victims of child maltreatment peaked in the early to mid 1990s when roughly 1 million children were reported to be victims of child abuse or neglect annually. From the later 1990s through FY2006, roughly 900,000 children were reported in each year to be victims of abuse or neglect; this translated to a rate of roughly

12 victims of child maltreatment for every 1,000 children in the population. For FY2007, however, the number of reported child maltreatment victims declined to 794,000—or less than 11 victims for every 1,000 children in the population.

HHS attributes the decline in the number of victims reported in FY2007 to 1) an increase in the number of children with the investigation/assessment finding of "other" (these children are not counted as victims); 2) a decrease in the number of children with findings of "substantiated" or "indicated" (these children are counted as victims); and 3) a decrease in the number of children who received an investigation or assessment.[23] The reason for all of these changes is not entirely clear. However, some states reported differences in how they collected and/or reported child maltreatment data for FY2007, and these changes may be largely responsible for the change in the national number of child maltreatment reports and of victims.[24] (For a table showing, on a national basis, the number and rate of children who were the subject of a child abuse or neglect investigation, see Appendix C.)

Types of Child Maltreatment

Children experience neglect far more than any other type of maltreatment. Among the 794,000 children counted as victims of child abuse or neglect in FY2007, 59% were reported as having experienced neglect only (including medical neglect), about 11% were reported as victims of physical abuse only, and less than 8% were reported as victims of sexual abuse only. In addition, about 13% were found to have experienced two or more types of maltreatment (e.g., the child experienced both neglect and physical abuse). There has been a decline in the reported rates of physical abuse and sexual abuse over roughly the past 15 years.[25] (For a table showing trends in the share of child victims by maltreatment type, see Appendix C.)

Age and Race/Ethnicity of Child Maltreatment Victims

States report the highest rates of child maltreatment among young children and among children who are African-American, American Indian/Alaska Native, or reported as being of two or more races.

Infants and young children are the least able to care for and protect themselves and are more likely to be determined victims of child abuse or neglect than are older children. In FY2007, nearly 22 infants (children under the age of one year) were found to be victims of child maltreatment for every 1,000 infants in the population. By contrast, for FY2007, the child maltreatment rate reported for children ages one or two years was sharply below that of infants, at 13 for every 1,000 children of that age in the population; for three to seven years olds, the comparable rate was just below 12; for eight to 15 year olds, it was roughly nine; and for 16 and 17 year olds, it was five.

The 1st, 2nd, and 3rd National Incidence Surveys, which studied the incidence of child abuse and neglect in the general population, found no direct link between race and child maltreatment; however, certain racial groups are disproportionately likely to be counted as victims of child abuse and neglect.[26] Across all race/ethnicities, less than 11 out of every 1,000 children in the population were reported by states as victims of child abuse or neglect in FY2007. However, the comparable rates for African Americans (16.7), American Indian/Alaska Native children (14.2), and children of two or more races (14.0) are higher than this overall rate, while the rates for white (9.1) and Hispanic children (10.3) are somewhat lower, and the rate for Asian children (2.4) is much lower.[27]

There are a variety of theories about why some children of color might be overrepresented in the child welfare system more generally, including disproportionate need (data show children of color are more likely to live in poor or single-parent homes, both of which have been associated with higher rates of child abuse or neglect); disproportionate attention (they come into contact with social service or other workers who notice and may be required to report suspected maltreatment); biased decision-making (they are more likely to be referred to CPS by those workers than are other children); and fewer community resources (they live in communities with fewer family support or other needed services).[28] These theories are not necessarily mutually exclusive and, to the extent they are true, might operate differently in different locations.

Post-Investigation Services

As discussed earlier, roughly three-fourths of all CPS agencies nationwide require investigators to provide short-term services to families, as needed, during child abuse and neglect investigations, and also to refer families for post-investigation services if needed.[29] Post-investigation services most often offered to families were parenting classes and substance abuse programs. Less frequently offered services included marital counseling, family system therapy, grief counseling, advocacy services, dental exams, homemaker/chore services, employment services, and financial planning.[30]

In recent years, roughly one in five of all children found to be victims of child abuse or neglect were removed from their homes within 90 days of the investigation. During that same time period, about two in five children found to be victims of abuse or neglect received some services while they remained living in their homes, and the remaining two in five identified victims did not receive any additional services following the close of the investigation. A child maltreatment victim may not receive post-investigation services if the child's and family's needs were met during the investigation. Others may not be served because services are not available or the waiting list for them is very long.[31] Finally, children who are not found to be victims of abuse or neglect may nonetheless be determined to be in need of post-investigation services. In recent years, roughly one out of four "non-victims" received some services following an investigation (while they remained in their home) and a small percentage were removed from their homes. (For a table estimating receipt of post-investigation services, nationally, by a child's status as "victim" or "non-victim," see Appendix D.)

Risk of Poor Child and Family Outcomes among Families Where an Investigation of Abuse or Neglect Occurs

In recent years, CPS workers have conducted roughly 1.9 to 2.0 million child abuse or neglect investigations (or assessments) annually, typically involving as many as 3.5 or 3.6 million children. Findings from a nationally representative survey of children in families investigated for abuse or neglect show that this population is at risk of poor child and family outcomes, regardless of whether the investigation determines the child to be a victim.[32]

Family and Caregiver Risk Factors

Many families visited by CPS workers face challenges to their stability, which might limit their ability to nurture and adequately support their children. Caseworkers reported that more than half of the families (54%) included in the nationally representative survey of children in families investigated for abuse or neglect had only one supportive caregiver in the home, close to one-third (31%) were assessed as having low social support, and nearly one-quarter had trouble paying for basic necessities. Caseworkers also identified poor parenting, serious mental health problems, domestic violence, and abuse of alcohol and drugs as issues facing significant numbers of families investigated for abuse or neglect. Notably, many of these families had prior contact with

CPS. A little more than half (51%) had been the subject of prior reports of abuse or neglect, one-quarter had a prior incident of substantiated child abuse and neglect, and close to 30% had previously been served by the child welfare agency (not including investigation as a service).[33] The percentages cited here represent the share of risk factors *among all families* where an investigation occurred. In general, the share of families experiencing these risk factors was higher among those who received services following the investigation and was highest among families where a child was removed from the home following the investigation. (See Appendix B for a table showing the percentage of families/caregivers that experienced these risk factors, as assessed by the CPS investigator, based on level of service subsequently received.)

Not surprisingly, high cumulative caregiver/parent risk factors (as assessed by the CPS investigator) predicted placement in out-of-home care or receipt of services while the child remained in the home. (Findings displayed in this report did not show presence of risk factors by whether or not a child was determined to have been a substantiated victim of abuse or neglect.) In addition, investigative caseworkers most often cited two factors, a "reasonable level of caregiver cooperation" and "child's inability to self protect," as critical in their decision-making process. Caregiver cooperation was especially influential in cases where a CPS worker decided the child should remain at home. A child's inability to self protect was most significant in decision-making with regard to younger children. For older children, however, investigative caseworkers cited the importance of the child's special health or other needs.[34]

Risk Factors among Children

Children in families investigated for abuse or neglect exhibit a greater risk for developmental delays and behavior problems than do children in the general population. This higher risk appears to exist across the range of children in families investigated for abuse and neglect and is not necessarily limited to those families in which the allegation of abuse or neglect is "substantiated" or to those children who are removed from their homes following an investigation.

School-age children who were in families investigated for abuse or neglect were at least twice as likely as children in the general population to be identified (using a standardized checklist) as having clinical or borderline clinical levels of problem behavior. In addition, they scored comparatively lower on reading and (especially) math scores, and social and living skills, and exhibited higher levels of depression.[35]

Under CAPTA, states are required to have procedures in place to refer children who are found to be substantiated victims of child abuse or neglect for screening under the Part C, early intervention services, program that is part of the Individuals with Disabilities Education Act (IDEA).[36] Analyzing survey data among the nationally representative sample of children in families investigated for abuse or neglect, researchers determined that as many as 34% of the youngest children in these families (those under age three) *had a developmental delay* that would qualify them for special education services under the eligibility criteria used in most states for the Part C program. The comparable percentages among the general population for children with developmental delay is 2% to 23%, depending on the study used.[37]

The researchers also found that the presence of developmental delay was not limited to young children who were determined to be victims of child abuse and neglect. Rather, they reported: "Children with unsubstantiated reports [of child abuse or neglect] (38%) were significantly more likely than children with substantiated reports (28%) to be in need of Part C services due to developmental delay or an established medical condition." At the same time, they noted that children with unsubstantiated reports of child abuse or neglect were less likely to receive services than children substantiated as victims of abuse or neglect. The degree to which the child welfare agency should play a role in service access for all children it investigates, regardless of substantiation status, is an important area for future research and policy consideration, the researchers stated.[38] (For tables showing prevalence of certain risk factors among children in families investigated for child abuse and neglect, and, separately, family or caregiver risk factors in that population, see Appendix B.)

The remainder of this report discusses grants programs and other activities authorized by CAPTA, including the funding provided and authorized for them.

CAPTA Grants and Activities

The well-being of children is the subject of a range of federal programs that are collectively referred to as "child welfare" programs.[39] The primary goals of federal child welfare programs are to ensure the safety of children; to enable them to be part of strong, permanent families; and, in doing this, to foster the well-being of children and their families. CAPTA is the only federal child welfare program focused solely on preventing child abuse or neglect as well as responding to allegations of abuse or neglect. As such, it is a critical piece of federal child welfare policy related to ensuring children's safety. In addition, efforts to prevent child abuse or neglect or to ensure that children may safely remain in a home where child abuse or neglect has been alleged are critical to the goal of permanence. The remainder of this report discusses activities authorized and required under CAPTA and funds provided. Table 1 provides a snapshot of the programs or activities authorized under CAPTA, including use of funds, requirements, and funding.

Table 1. The Child Abuse Prevention and Treatment Act (CAPTA) At a Glance

Program or Activity	Use of Funds and Related Requirements	Funding and Current Distribution Practice
State Grants to Improve Child Protective Services (Section 106 of CAPTA)	Funds are provided to state child welfare agencies and may be used to improve its system of child protective services (CPS). To receive these funds, a state must provide assurances that it has procedures or policies 1) to receive and respond to allega-tions of child abuse or neglect, ensure children's safety, and provide appropriate referrals; 2) for the appointment of an appropriately trained guardian ad litem (attorney or volunteer) for each child victim involved in a court proceeding; 3) to main-tain confidentiality of child abuse and neglect records; and 4) for improving training to workers. States are also required to establish and support Citizen Review Panels to evaluate the effectiveness of CPS policies and practices and must, "to the maximum extent practicable," submit certain child abuse and neglect data to HHS each year.	FY2009 funding was $26.5 million. Funding authorization (under Section 112 of CAPTA) expired with FY2008 but Congress has conti-nued annual funding. Each eligible state rec-eives a base allotment of $50,000; remaining funds are distributed in roportion to each state's relative share of the child population among all eligible states. The median grant in FY2009 was $367,000.

Table 1. (Continued)

Program or Activity	Use of Funds and Related Requirements	Funding and Current Distribution Practice
	For FY2008, states, as a whole, planned to spend about half of these funds (48%) for prevention related services, a little less than that (44%) for investigations and related services, 5% for training, and the remainder for intensive family preservation or efforts to reunite children with their parents.	
Research, Demonstration, and Technical Assistance (Sections 101-105 of CAPTA)	Funds are awarded competitively to support an ongoing research program and other work related to better identifying, preventing, and treating child abuse and neglect and for required federal efforts to collect and disseminate child abuse and neglect data, operate an information clearinghouse, and provide technical assistance related to child abuse and neglect prevention and treatment. A few of the projects and activities currently funded (in whole or part) include the Child Welfare Information Gateway website, annual publication of *Child Maltreatment,* the National Resource Center for Child Protective Services, the National Quality Improvement Center on Differential Response, and the initiative on Supporting Evidence-Based Home Visitation to Prevent Child Maltreatment.	FY2009 funding for these activities was $41.8 million. Funding authorization (under Section 112 of CAPTA) expired with FY2008 but Congress has continued annual funding. Funds are awarded by HHS via grants, contracts, or ooperative agreements.

Table 1. (Continued)

Program or Activity	Use of Funds and Related Requirements	Funding and Current Distribution Practice
Community-Based Grants for the Prevention of Child Abuse or Neglect (Title II of CAPTA)	Funds are provided to a designated lead entity in each state for support and development of community-based programs and activities that prevent child abuse and neglect. The lead entity must make an inventory of unmet preventive services needs in the state, foster a continuum of family support and strengthening services at the community level, leverage non-federal funds to support prevention programs and activities, and provide technical assistance to funded community-based groups. Community-based groups that receive sub-grants from the lead entity must provide, directly or by referral, core family resource and family support services. These services include parent education and parent mutual support groups, community and social service referrals, voluntary home visiting, and respite care.	FY2009 funding was $41.7 million. Funding authorization (under Section 210 of CAPTA) expired with FY2008 but Congress has continued annual funding. Seventy percent of the funding is allotted to a state in proportion to its share of the child population, except that no state may receive less than $200,000. The remaining 30% is distributed to a state based on its share of the total pot of *non-federal funds* leveraged by states for use under this program. The median grant in FY2009 was $567,000.
"Children's Justice Act" Grants (Section 107 of CAPTA)	Funds are made available to each state to improve systems related to the investigation, prosecution, and overall handling of child abuse and neglect cases with particular focus on cases involving child sexual abuse and exploitation, child abuse or neglect related fatalities, or maltreatment of children with disabilities.	FY2009 funding was $20 million (of which $3 million was reserved for tribal use). Up to $20 million in funding is required to be set aside annually from the Crime Victims Fund (Sections 1402(d) and 1404A of

Table 1. (Continued)

Program or Activity	Use of Funds and Related Requirements	Funding and Current Distribution Practice
	To receive these funds, a state must establish a multi-disciplinary task force to study state administrative, judicial, and investigative practice related to child abuse and neglect cases; receive recommendations from this taskforce in the initial year that grants are funded (and every three years after); and implement those recommendations (or an alternative plan). In addition, a state must meet all the requirements for receipt of CAPTA state grants.	the Victims of Crime Act) Funds are distributed in the same manner as the CAPTA State Grant. The median grant in FY2009 was $238,000.

Source: Table prepared by the Congressional Research Service.

State Grants

Funding for CAPTA state grants ($26.5 million in FY2009) is provided to help states improve their CPS systems and may be used for a range of purposes specified in the law. To be eligible to receive these state grant funds, a state must submit a plan including certain assurances related to how it will operate its CPS system; establish and support citizen review panels; and, to the "maximum extent practicable," annually supply to HHS certain child abuse and neglect data. The statute provides that any funds appropriated for these purposes must be distributed to all eligible states by formula.

Allowable Use of Funds

CAPTA state grant funds are intended to improve the state CPS system, and the statute provides a variety of areas in which they can be used to make improvements.[40] These are:

- ***Receipt and investigation of reports of child abuse and neglect:*** Educate the public on the role of CPS and the nature and basis for reporting child abuse and neglect; develop and facilitate research-based training protocols for individuals mandated to report child abuse or neglect; improve intake assessment, screening, and investigation of reports; develop, improve, and implement risk and safety assessment tools and protocols; and improve and enhance investigation of child abuse and neglect reports by creating multidisciplinary teams and interagency protocols.

- ***Prevention and services:*** Improve case management, including ongoing case monitoring, and delivery of services and treatment to children and their families; develop and enhance the capacity of community-based programs to prevent and treat child abuse and neglect and to integrate parent and professional leadership strategies to do so; and develop, implement, or operate programs to assist in obtaining or coordinating necessary services for families of disabled infants with life-threatening conditions.
- ***Training and workforce recruitment and retention:*** Develop, strengthen, and facilitate training, including training on research-based strategies to promote collaboration with families, the legal duties (of CPS workers),[41] and personal safety for case workers; and improve the skills, qualifications, and availability of individuals providing services to children and families through the child protection system, and the supervisors of such individuals.
- ***Collaboration between agencies:*** Support and enhance interagency collaboration between the child protection system and the juvenile justice system to improve services and treatment, and provide methods for continuity of treatment plans and services for children moving between the systems; and support and enhance collaboration among public health agencies, CPS agencies, and private community-based programs to provide child abuse and neglect prevention and treatment services (including linkages with education systems) and to address the health needs, including mental health needs, of children identified as abused or neglected, including supporting prompt comprehensive health and developmental evaluations for children who are the subject of substantiated child maltreatment reports.
- ***Legal preparation and representation:*** Improve legal preparation and representation, including procedures for appealing and responding to appeals of substantiated reports of child abuse and neglect and provision for the appointment of an appropriately trained individual to represent the best interests of child victims in judicial proceedings.

- ***Data collection:*** Develop and update technology systems that support the work of the CPS agency, track reports of child abuse and neglect from intake through final disposition, and allow interstate and intrastate information exchange.

Requirements for Receipt of State Grant Funds

All 50 states, the District of Columbia, Puerto Rico, and other territories receive CAPTA state grants. To receive these funds, states (including the District of Columbia and Puerto Rico) must submit an initial application as well as a renewal application no less often than every five years.[42] Under regulations provided by HHS, the application is to be submitted as part of a broader Child and Family Services Plan (CFSP) that is intended to encourage the integration of several federal programs that provide funds for services to children and their families.[43] The CAPTA state grant application must include a state plan for the CAPTA grant program, which is discussed in more detail below.

Description of Use of Funds and Program Coordination

In its plan, a state must outline how it intends to spend CAPTA state grant funds, including specifying what areas of its CPS system it will seek to improve, and what child abuse prevention services will be provided (directly or through referral). Further, states must, "to the maximum extent practicable," coordinate the CAPTA state grant program with the federal Stephanie Tubbs Jones Child Welfare Services and Promoting Safe and Stable Families programs. Those programs are authorized under Title IV-B of the Social Security Act and provide formula funding to all states for a range of services to children and families.[44] Accordingly, in their CAPTA state grant plan, states must certify that any activities that are related to preventing, responding to, or treating child abuse or neglect and that are carried out under those Title IV-B programs meet the requirements for CAPTA state grants.[45] The CAPTA state plan must further describe training to be provided for mandatory reporters of child abuse and neglect, as well as training for CPS workers. Finally, states are required to notify HHS annually about any substantive changes in state law that could affect their eligibility for CAPTA state grant funds and any significant changes in how the grant funds will be used.

Assurances

To receive CAPTA state grant funding, a state must also provide assurances in its state plan that it has in effect a statewide policy or program, or is enforcing a statewide law related to child abuse and neglect in the following areas:

- ***Receiving, screening, and investigating allegations of child abuse and neglect:*** A state must have procedures to receive reports of known or suspected child abuse and neglect, and for the immediate screening, risk and safety assessment, and investigation of those reports.[46] These procedures must include a requirement that health care providers who are involved in the delivery or care of an infant who has been affected by prenatal exposure to illegal substances notify CPS of the infant's condition.[47] Further, they must provide that designated individuals at health care facilities promptly notify CPS of suspected medical neglect and that the state CPS have procedures for coordinating and consulting with those individuals on all cases of reported medical neglect.[48] With regard to each investigation (or assessment) of reported child abuse and neglect, the state must require that a CPS worker, at the initial time of contact with the alleged perpetrator, advise that individual of the allegations made against him or her and do this in a manner consistent with laws that protect the rights of the person who made the allegation of abuse or neglect. The state must also have provisions by which individuals who disagree with an official finding of abuse or neglect can appeal this finding.[49] Further, the state must provide, by law and regulation, for the immunity from prosecution of any individual making a good faith report of suspected instances of child abuse or neglect.[50]
- ***Ensuring children's safety and making referrals to other services:*** A state must have procedures to refer children not at risk of imminent harm to a community organization or voluntary preventive service. A state must also have procedures to immediately ensure the safety of any child who is abused or neglected, as well as any child who may be at risk of abuse or neglect by the same caretaker, and to ensure children's placement in a safe environment.[51] Special procedures or laws must be in place to respond to 1) child maltreatment victims under three years of age (i.e., the state must have provisions for their referral to early intervention services under Part C of the Individuals with Disabilities Education Act); 2) for infants identified as being affected by prenatal exposure to illegal substances (i.e., the state must have provisions for development of a plan of safe care); and 3) for cases involving medical neglect (i.e., the state must have a law that

grants CPS the authority to pursue legal remedies, including those necessary to provide medical care or treatment when necessary).[52]

- ***Legal representation of children in abuse and neglect judicial proceedings:*** States are required to have provisions for the appointment of an appropriately trained guardian ad litem (an attorney, court-appointed special advocate, or both) to represent each child abuse or neglect victim who is involved in a judicial proceeding.[53]
- ***Confidentiality of records:*** In general, states must maintain the confidentiality of all records and reports related to their child abuse and neglect investigations. At the same time, a state *must* have procedures to release information from these confidential records to any federal, state, or local government entity, or an agent of these entities, that needs this information to carry out its responsibilities under law to protect children from abuse and neglect. Two of these entities, child fatality review panels and citizen review panels, are specifically named in the statute and must be given access to confidential information needed to perform their work. Further, the state is *required* to release to the public information concerning a child abuse and neglect case when it resulted in the death or near death of a child.

  States are *permitted* to release child abuse and neglect records to 1) individuals who are the subject of a report; 2) a grand jury or court, if the information in the record is necessary to determine an issue before the grand jury or court; and 3) any other entity or class of individuals that is authorized *by state law* to receive the information for a legitimate state purpose (e.g., researchers, or employers conducting background checks). Finally, a state is also *permitted* to allow public access to child abuse and neglect court proceedings, provided that it does so in a manner that ensures the safety and well-being of the child, parent, and families.[54] Individuals or entities who receive confidential information from a child abuse and neglect case are bound by the same confidentiality rules as the state and may not re-release the information.[55] In the case of citizen review panel members, a state must have in place civil sanctions for any member of a panel that re-discloses identifying or other information from a CPS case without specific authorization to do so.[56]

  States must also have procedures to expunge any records made available to the general public or used for purposes of employment or other background checks in cases where the child abuse or neglect allegation is unsubstantiated or found to be false. This requirement, however, does not preclude state CPS agencies from keeping information on unsubstantiated cases in its casework files to assist in future risk and safety assessments.[57] Finally, unless it is ordered to do so by a court, a state is always permitted to refuse to disclose identifying information concerning the person who made a specific allegation of child abuse or neglect.[58]

- ***Training, worker retention, and supervision:*** In addition to describing training programs for CPS workers and mandatory reporters in their state plan (see "Description of Use of Funds and Program Coordination"), states are required to have provisions to improve the training of caseworkers, as well as methods for training or informing CPS workers regarding their legal duties ("in order to protect the legal rights and safety of children and families from the initial time of contact during investigation through treatment"). States must also have provisions related to improving retention and supervision of caseworkers.[59]
- ***Establishment and support of citizen review panels:*** States are required to establish no less than three citizen review panels (or no less than one in less populous states).[60] The panels must be composed of volunteers who are "broadly representative" of the community, including members with expertise in the prevention and treatment of child abuse and neglect, and may include foster care review boards or child fatality panels. Citizen review panels are required to meet at least once every three months and to evaluate the effectiveness of state and local CPS agencies' policies and practices in protecting children. As part of doing this work, they must provide for public outreach and comment on the impact of CPS work. Each panel must provide to the state an annual written report (which also must be made available to the public) that summarizes its activities and recommendations for CPS improvements at the state and local level. Within six months of receiving the report, the state must submit a written response to the citizen review panel and to state and local child protection systems that describes whether or how the state will incorporate the recommendations of the panel. Finally, to permit citizen review panels to carry out their duties, states must grant them access to information on cases that the panels wish to review and must

also provide, as requested, staff assistance to help the panels carry out their duties.[61]

- ***Termination of parental rights:*** Termination of parental rights is a legal process that severs the legal relationship (rights and responsibilities) between a parent and child. As part of ensuring children's safety and permanency, states are required to have provisions for the expedited termination of parental rights in the case of an infant who has been abandoned. States must also have provisions ensuring that no child whose parent has been convicted of a heinous crime against that child or a sibling of that child (e.g., murder, voluntary manslaughter, conspiracy to murder, or felony assault resulting in serious bodily injury to the child or sibling) be required to be reunited with that parent. In addition, once a state has those provisions in place, it must establish by state law that those same crimes against the child (or a sibling of the child) are grounds for termination of parental rights. At the same time, case-by-case determinations of whether to seek termination of parental rights remain, under CAPTA statute, at the sole discretion of the state.[62]
- ***Criminal background checks:*** States are required to ensure that criminal background checks are completed for every prospective foster or adoptive parent and for any other adult(s) living in the household.[63]

Data Reporting

States must, "to the maximum extent practicable," report certain child abuse and neglect data to HHS. Specifically, these data are 1) the number of children who were reported to the state during the year as abused or neglected and, of those children, the number for whom the report was substantiated, unsubstantiated, or determined to be false; 2) the number of children reported as abused or neglect who received services under CAPTA (or an equivalent state program) during the year, the number who did not, and the number who were removed from their families; 3) the number of children reunited with their families, or receiving family preservation services, that within five years were the subject of a subsequent substantiated report of child abuse or neglect (including death); 4) the number of deaths in the state during the year that were the result of child abuse or neglect and the number of those deaths that involved children in foster care; 5) the number of children for whom individuals were appointed by the court to represent the children's best interests and the average number of out-of-court contacts between the appointed representatives and these children; 6) the number of children "under the care of the state child protection system" whose custody is transferred to the state juvenile justice system; 7) the number of families that received preventive services during the year; 8) the number of CPS workers responsible for intake and screening of child abuse and neglect reports, and the number of those same CPS workers, as well as the number of CPS investigators, relative to the number of reports investigated; and 9) the agency response time with respect to initial investigation of child abuse or neglect and the response time with respect to the provision of services to families where an allegation of abuse or neglect has been made. Finally, states must, to the maximum extent practicable, submit to HHS the annual report summarizing the activities of their citizen review panels.[64]

Distribution of State Grant Funds

HHS awards CAPTA state grants to each of the 50 states, the District of Columbia, Puerto Rico, American Samoa, Guam, the Northern Mariana Islands, and the U.S. Virgin Islands. Each of these 56 jurisdictions receives a base allotment of $50,000, after which the remaining funds are allocated to each jurisdiction based on its relative share of the child (under age 18) population among all of those jurisdictions. No matching funds are required to receive this grant.[65] The statute does not authorize distribution of CAPTA state grants to Indian tribes or tribal organizations.[66] CAPTA state grant amounts among the 50 states, the District of Columbia, and Puerto Rico ranged from a low of $85,000 to a high of just over $3.0 million in FY2009. The median grant among those 52 jurisdictions was $367,000. Table 2 shows CAPTA state grant funding for each of FY2007-FY2009 by state.

Reported Use of Funds

As part of their FY2008 application to receive these grants, states reported that they planned to spend close to half of their CAPTA state grant funds (48%) on prevention and support services (these might include respite care, early developmental screening of children, services to increase parenting skills, home visiting, and family support or resource centers); a little less than that (44%) for protective services (which, among other things, includes investigations, case management, and service referrals); 5% for training; and the remainder on intensive family preservation or services to expeditiously reunite children removed from their homes with their parents.[67]

Table 2. CAPTA State Grant Funding, By State

State	FY2007	FY2008	FY2009
Alabama	$403,461	$403,469	$405,387
Alaska	$111,083	$106,929	$107,637
Arizona	$562,613	$565,425	$578,195
Arkansas	$269,137	$269,570	$271,587
California	$3,196,791	$3,069,656	$3,018,231
Colorado	$432,902	$420,570	$427,257
Connecticut	$320,834	$309,119	$309,443
Delaware	$113,533	$114,548	$115,048
District of Columbia	$86,599	$86,381	$85,971
Florida	$1,369,413	$1,323,199	$1,329,020
Georgia	$816,347	$826,922	$850,774
Hawaii	$147,257	$144,170	$140,368
Idaho	$171,365	$174,928	$178,963
Illinois	$1,101,228	$1,069,026	$1,061,927
Indiana	$569,882	$550,453	$551,832
Iowa	$267,574	$276,376	$275,024
Kansas	$268,055	$270,087	$270,178
Kentucky	$367,914	$366,931	$367,567
Louisiana	$422,240	$395,019	$391,476
Maine	$139,954	$139,304	$138,398
Maryland	$505,049	$481,555	$479,801
Massachusetts	$522,913	$508,911	$503,227
Michigan	$868,746	$834,904	$823,966
Minnesota	$448,813	$448,541	$448,640
Mississippi	$292,790	$290,446	$293,149
Missouri	$497,029	$500,658	$500,688
Montana	$116,490	$119,098	$119,429
Nebraska	$189,999	$191,116	$191,120
Nevada	$251,479	$251,007	$258,765
New Hampshire	$148,327	$144,311	$144,319
New Jersey	$751,179	$712,050	$702,798
New Mexico	$208,763	$211,691	$208,242
New York	$1,524,454	$1,479,978	$1,446,008
North Carolina	$744,445	$732,760	$751,475

Table 2. (Continued)

State	FY2007	FY2008	FY2009
North Dakota	$94,280	$95,500	$95,172
Ohio	$944,916	$928,480	$920,446
Oklahoma	$326,779	$333,616	$334,523
Oregon	$325,679	$321,713	$322,947
Pennsylvania	$963,607	$939,492	$931,468
Puerto Rico	$384,763	$372,734	$367,241
Rhode Island	$129,580	$125,229	$123,737
South Carolina	$383,172	$379,137	$385,263
South Dakota	$111,065	$111,456	$112,278
Tennessee	$501,015	$508,459	$515,446
Texas	$2,101,926	$2,110,255	$2,145,039
Utah	$290,848	$300,978	$308,369
Vermont	$93,015	$92,424	$91,548
Virginia	$641,797	$622,041	$627,639
Washington	$531,453	$534,066	$535,969
West Virginia	$174,063	$173,631	$172,533
Wisconsin	$470,355	$466,604	$467,934
Wyoming	$87,080	$88,313	$89,654
50 states, DC, and Puerto Rico subtotal	***$26,764,051***	***$26,293,236***	***$26,293,116***
Insular Areas (consolidated grants)[a]			
American Samoa	$58,283	$58,091	$58,078
Guam	$67,792	$67,379	$67,351
Northern Mariana Islands	$55,752	$55,618	$55,609
U.S. Virgin Islands	$61,122	$60,864	$60,846
Insular areas subtotal	***$242,949***	***$241,952***	***$241,884***
TOTAL	**$27,007,000**	**$26,535,188**	**$26,535,000**

Source: Table prepared by the Congressional Research Service.

a. These territories are referred to here as "insular areas" because this is the term used in federal regulation (45 CFR Part 97), which permits them to submit a consolidated grant application for these grants and for grants under other social services programs. Under this regulation, these jurisdictions must meet only those program requirements specified in the consolidated grant application for which they intend to use the funds.

Funds provided under CAPTA state grants may support improved prevention activities in the state and improvements to the CPS system for receiving and responding to reports of abuse or neglect.

Title II of CAPTA exclusively provides funds to support community-based child abuse or neglect prevention activities. No federal program, however, exclusively provides funds for the *operation* of state CPS systems, although states may, and do, use a variety of federal funding streams to support their CPS systems (including, for example, funding under the Social Services Block Grant (SSBG), Temporary Assistance for Needy Families (TANF) block grant, and the Stephanie Tubbs Jones Child Welfare Services program). Available data, however, suggest that states provide the largest share of CPS funding from non-federal sources (state and local dollars). For FY2007 (most recent data available), states reported spending $270 million through the SSBG funding stream (including TANF funds transferred to that block grant) [68] for "child protective services."[69] However, among the 36 states able to report on total child protective services spending in their state, SSBG spending amounted to less than 8% of all state spending (including state, local, and federal dollars) for child protective services.[70]

Community-Based Grants to Prevent Child Abuse and Neglect

CAPTA Title II community-based grants— administratively referred to as Community-Based grants for Child Abuse Prevention or CBCAP grants—are one of the few sources of federal child and family services funding that are wholly dedicated to the prevention of child abuse and neglect. The funds are distributed to a state-designated lead entity in each state, and must be redistributed by that lead entity to community-based groups for the support of a continuum of prevention-focused programs and activities designed to strengthen and support families to prevent child abuse and neglect. Programs and activities supported may range from public campaigns to prevent child abuse or neglect to provision of services for families such as home visiting, respite care, and parenting education. Families served with CBCAP funds are typically those that meet some "at risk" definition but—in keeping with the prevention focus—are not in current contact with the child welfare agency. The statute directs that some of the CBCAP funds be set aside for technical assistance and for tribal or migrant programs before distribution to all states. The distribution is based, in part, on each state's relative share of child population as well as its ability to leverage non-federal funds to further support prevention activities and services.

Allowable Use of Funds

The statute stipulates how the state-designated lead entity must use CBCAP funds and also provides certain complementary requirements for the use of funds by community-based sub-grantees. CBCAP funds are to be used by the state's lead entity for the following purposes.[71]

- ***Develop, operate, expand, and enhance community-based, prevention-focused programs and activities designed to strengthen and support families to prevent child abuse and neglect.*** Programs and activities are expected to be accessible, effective, and culturally appropriate, and to 1) offer support to families to increase family stability and improve access to services; 2) promote the development of parenting skills (especially in young parents and parents with young children); 3) demonstrate a commitment to meaningful parent leadership in the planning for and operation of community-based programs; and 4) support the additional needs of families that include children with disabilities (through respite care and other services). Finally, in awarding grants to community-based programs, the lead entity must give priority to effective programs that serve low-income communities, and those that serve young parents or parents with young children, including community-based family resource and support programs.
- ***Foster a continuum of prevention services for children and families*** through state and community-based collaborations and partnerships, both public and private.
- ***Finance the start-up and operation of family support and family resource services that respond to identified unmet needs.*** Unmet needs are to be identified by a regular inventory of community-based services.
- ***Maximize funding for services to strengthen and support families to prevent child abuse and neglect*** by leveraging and integrating all available public and private funds at the federal, state, and local levels.
- ***Finance public information campaigns*** focused on health and positive development of parents and children and on the prevention of child abuse and neglect.

Community-based groups receiving funds via the state entity must focus on similar activities at the local level.[72] These are 1) assessing community need and involving parents in planning a continuum of services; 2) developing a strategy to provide, over time, a continuum of services through public and private partnerships; 3) providing core family resource and family support services, including services related to parent education, mutual support, and self help; outreach services; and community and social service referrals; 4) providing, or arranging for provision of, other core services, including voluntary home visiting and all forms of respite care services[73]; 5) developing leadership roles for meaningful involvement of parents in designing, operating, evaluating, and overseeing these prevention and support programs and services; 6) providing leadership in mobilizing local public and private resources for these services; and 7) participating with other community-based groups and activities to strengthen prevention activities and family resources and supports.

Eligibility Requirements

To be eligible for funding, a state must designate a lead entity to direct CBCAP funding and efforts; provide certain assurances, including some related to the qualifications and work of that lead entity; submit an application that includes a description of certain planned CBCAP activities, a budget showing that the state will provide not less than 20% in matching program funds, and other assurances; and submit annual program reports to HHS.

- ***Designate a lead entity to direct the spending of CBCAP funds.*** The entity selected may be a public, private nonprofit, or quasi-public organization. It must have a demonstrated ability to integrate child abuse and neglect prevention services and activities and to leverage and blend a variety of funds to support these activities.[74] In roughly half of the states (including Puerto Rico), a public agency serves as the lead entity (most commonly the child welfare agency or another agency within the human services department),[75] and in the remaining states (including the District of Columbia), quasi-public or private nonprofit agencies (most commonly the state's Children's Trust Fund) have been designated as the lead entity.[76]
- ***Assurances concerning the work of the lead entity.*** The state must provide assurances that the lead entity will provide, or be responsible for, 1) community-based and prevention-focused programs and activities designed to strengthen and support families and to prevent

child abuse and neglect, and that these programs, where appropriate, will be provided through a network;[77] 2) direction through an interdisciplinary and collaborative public-private structure that includes balanced representation from public and private sector members, parents (including parents with disabilities), and nonprofit and public service providers; 3) direction and oversight by identifying goals and objectives; 4) clear lines of communication and accountability; 5) leveraged or combined funding from federal, state, local, and private sources; 6) centralized assessment and planning activities; 7) training and technical assistance; and 8) reporting and evaluation. Further, the state must assure that the lead entity will integrate its efforts with the child abuse and neglect activities of the state and with individuals and organizations experienced in working in partnership with families that have children with disabilities and parents with disabilities.[78]

- ***Assurances concerning the qualifications of the lead entity.*** The state must provide assurances that the lead entity it designates has 1) a demonstrated commitment to involving parents in the development, operation, and oversight of community-based programs that support families to prevent child abuse and neglect; 2) shown its ability to work with state and community-based organizations (both public and private nonprofit groups) to develop a continuum of preventive services and supports for children and families; and 3) the capacity, through interagency funding and interdisciplinary service delivery mechanisms, to provide operational support (financial and programmatic), training, and technical assistance to community-based child abuse prevention and family resource and support programs.[79]
- ***Submit an application including descriptions, assurances, and plans related to administration of CBCAP and the role of the lead entity.*** The state must submit an application to HHS that 1) describes the lead entity that will be responsible for administration of the CBCAP grant and oversight of the community-based programs funded; 2) describes how those community-based programs will operate and how public and private family resource and support services will be integrated into developing a continuum of family-centered, holistic preventive services for children and families; 3) includes a plan for providing operational support, training, and technical assistance to community-based prevention programs to develop, operate, expand, and enhance their activities; 5) provides an inventory of community-based child

abuse and neglect prevention and family resource programs operating in the state and current unmet needs; 6) describes the criteria the lead entity will use to develop or to select and fund community-based child abuse and neglect prevention programs; 7) describes how the lead entity will advocate for systemic changes in state policy, practices, procedures, and regulations to improve the delivery of community-based, prevention-focused services to children and families; 8) describes the outreach activities that the lead entity and the community-based child abuse and neglect prevention programs will do to maximize the participation of racial and ethnic minorities, children and adults with disabilities, homeless families and those at risk of homelessness, and members of other underserved or underrepresented groups; and 9) assures that the state can meaningfully involve parents in planning, implementing, and evaluating programs and policy decisions of the lead entity.[80]

- ***Submit a program budget.*** As part of its application, the state must also supply HHS with a CBCAP program budget and it must verify that it will spend in nonfederal funds (cash only) an amount not less than 20% of its federal CBCAP funding. Further, the state must assure that federal CBCAP funds will be used to supplement, not supplant, other funds for community-based, prevention-focused programs serving children and families.[81]
- ***Provide performance and other reports or information deemed necessary by HHS.*** The application must describe how the work of the lead entity and of the community-based programs it funds will be evaluated. Further, the state must assure that it will provide HHS with annual reports on the program, including information on "performance measures" that 1) demonstrate that the state lead entity has effectively developed, operated, and expanded community-based programs that meet the requirements of CBCAP; 2) describe services provided by local programs and demonstrate that they have addressed identified unmet needs; 3) describe the number of families served and demonstrate their high level of satisfaction with the services; 4) describe the involvement of diverse families in designing, operating, and evaluating community-based programs to prevent child abuse and neglect and have an implementation plan to ensure continued leadership of parents in program design, operation, and evaluation; 5) demonstrate establishment or continuation of innovative funding mechanisms that blend a variety of resource and interdisciplinary

service mechanisms to develop, support, and expand community-based programs to prevent child abuse and neglect; and 6) describe the results of a peer review process conducted under the state program.[82]

Distribution of Funds

States that properly designate a lead entity, submit an application, and provide necessary reports and assurances are eligible to receive CBCAP funds. For FY2009, $41.7 million was appropriated for this grant program. The statute requires HHS to reserve 1% of the funds annually appropriated for grants to Indian tribes, tribal organizations, and migrant programs.[83] It further permits HHS to set aside "such sums as may be necessary" for certain program support and technical assistance activities.[84] Remaining funds are to be allocated among all states by formula.

- ***Tribal and migrant programs.*** The 1% reservation for tribal entities and migrant programs is distributed by HHS on a competitive basis. In FY2009, roughly $417,000 was available under this set-aside and the funds provided a second year of funding to three grantees: the Yakima Valley Farm Workers Clinic, Toppenish, WA; Grand Traverse Band of Ottawa and Chippewa Indians, Suttons Bay, MI; and the Indian Child Welfare Consortium, Temecula, CA. The grants are expected to extend for three years (FY2008-FY2010), and, contingent on the amount of appropriated funding, the annual support for grantees is anticipated to be just under $139,000 in each of those three years.
- ***Technical assistance and program support.*** As permitted by statute, the Children's Bureau also reserved some CBCAP funds (just under $1.5 million in FY2009) for ongoing support of the FRIENDS national resource center (http://www.friendsnrc.org), which supports CBCAP lead entities and the community-based programs they fund, and to provide additional technical assistance and program support.
- ***Funds to states.*** The remaining funds, approximately $40 million in FY2009, are distributed to all 50 states, the District of Columbia, Puerto Rico, American Samoa, Guam, the Northern Mariana Islands, and the U.S. Virgin Islands (56 jurisdictions) by formula.[85] Seventy percent of the funds (roughly $28 million in FY2009) are allotted to each jurisdiction based on its relative share of the total child (under age 18) population among all eligible jurisdictions. However, no

jurisdiction is permitted to receive less than a minimum allotment[86] of $200,000.[87] The remaining 30% of the CBCAP state funding (roughly $12 million in FY2009) is distributed based on the relative share of non-federal funds that a state (meaning the 50 states, the District of Columbia, and Puerto Rico) was able to leverage in support of child abuse and neglect prevention activities and services in the prior fiscal year. A state may claim as leveraged dollars any state, local, or private money used for CBCAP purposes, provided the funds were directed through the state's lead CBCAP entity[88] and were not used as matching funds or to meet maintenance of effort (MOE) requirements for any other federal program.[89]

As shown in Table 3, states leveraged more than $322 million in non-federal funding for child abuse and neglect prevention activities in FY2007, and a state's relative share of that total leveraged sum determined its share of the leverage funding awarded under the CBCAP program for FY2008. Table 3 also shows total CBCAP funds awarded to each state in FY2008, including the amounts of that award attributable to the state's relative share of the national child population (with a minimum allotment of $200,000) and to its share of total leveraged funds. Grant amounts to individual states ranged from about $200,000 on the low end to $3.6 million on the high end. The median grant (excluding the four territories) was $567,000.

Table 3. Community-Based Grants for the Prevention of Child Abuse and Neglect, FY2008 Awards

State	Award Based on Child Population	*Allowable Leveraged Funds Claimed*	*Share of Leverage Award*	Award Based on Leveraged Funds	TOTAL
Alabama	$380,295	*$2,000,000*	*0.62%*	$74,164	$454,459
Alaska	198,592	*1,074,474*	*0.33%*	39,843	238,435
Arizona	551,053	*13,780,331*	*4.28%*	511,000	1,062,053
Arkansas	238,086	*508,115*	*0.16%*	18,842	256,928
California	3,181,972	*12,356,000*	*3.84%*	458,183	3,640,155
Colorado	394,800	*8,913,178*	*2.77%*	330,517	725,317
Connecticut	264,562	*11,429,362*	*3.55%*	423,822	688,384
Delaware	203,009	*215,173*	*0.07%*	7,979	210,988
District of Columbia	199,409	*450,927*	*0.14%*	16,721	216,130
Florida	1,377,324	*590,232*	*0.18%*	21,887	1,399,211

Table 3. (Continued)

State	Award Based on Child Population	*Allowable Leveraged Funds Claimed*	*Share of Leverage Award*	Award Based on Leveraged Funds	TOTAL
Georgia	862,805	*0*	*0.00%*	0	862,805
Hawaii	182,281	*13,520,871*	*4.20%*	501,379	683,660
Idaho	199,894	*81,505*	*0.03%*	3,022	202,916
Illinois	1,087,985	*1,777,608*	*0.55%*	65,917	1,153,902
Indiana	693,069	*20,217,000*	*6.28%*	749,683	1,442,752
Iowa	230,761	*8,923,864*	*2.77%*	330,913	561,674
Kansas	217,950	*14,715,457*	*4.57%*	545,676	763,626
Kentucky	286,524	*42,459,678*	*13.18%*	1,574,482	1,861,006
Louisiana	366,740	*906,669*	*0.28%*	33,621	400,361
Maine	199,548	*345,216*	*0.11%*	12,801	212,349
Maryland	455,343	*5,916,079*	*1.84%*	219,379	674,722
Massachusetts	485,327	*2,296,115*	*0.71%*	85,144	570,471
Michigan	827,870	*4,616,802*	*1.43%*	171,199	999,069
Minnesota	396,343	*25,317,203*	*7.86%*	938,808	1,335,151
Mississippi	261,984	*0*	*0.00%*	0	261,984
Missouri	481,907	*2,818,908*	*0.88%*	104,530	586,437
Montana	199,947	*40,013*	*0.01%*	1,484	201,431
Nebraska	199,026	*743,488*	*0.23%*	27,570	226,596
Nevada	220,097	*3,693,227*	*1.15%*	136,952	357,049
New Hampshire	199,736	*201,376*	*0.06%*	7,467	207,203
New Jersey	655,667	*36,398,000*	*11.30%*	1,349,704	2,005,371
New Mexico	180,576	*14,821,568*	*4.60%*	549,611	730,187
New York	1,502,184	*1,499,765*	*0.47%*	55,614	1,557,798
North Carolina	745,330	*8,000,000*	*2.48%*	296,655	1,041,985
North Dakota	199,814	*142,200*	*0.04%*	5,273	205,087
Ohio	925,101	*9,747,657*	*3.03%*	361,461	1,286,562
Oklahoma	282,203	*18,588,934*	*5.77%*	689,312	971,515
Oregon	293,991	*75,122*	*0.02%*	2,786	296,777
Pennsylvania	947,675	*1,583,400*	*0.49%*	58,715	1,006,390
Puerto Rico	337,907	*2,983,158*	*0.93%*	110,621	448,528
Rhode Island	198,555	*1,102,718*	*0.34%*	40,891	239,446
South Carolina	361,126	*82,801*	*0.03%*	3,070	364,196
South Dakota	199,750	*190,529*	*0.06%*	7,065	206,815
Tennessee	484,569	*12,921,340*	*4.01%*	479,147	963,716
Texas	2,254,789	*1,938,371*	*0.60%*	71,878	2,326,667
Utah	273,965	*3,372,633*	*1.05%*	125,063	399,028
Vermont	196,150	*2,938,400*	*0.91%*	108,961	305,111
Virginia	621,764	*474,801*	*0.15%*	17,606	639,370
Washington	522,050	*1,193,279*	*0.37%*	44,249	566,299
West Virginia	198,099	*1,449,945*	*0.45%*	53,767	251,866

Table 3. (Continued)

State	Award Based on Child Population	*Allowable Leveraged Funds Claimed*	*Share of Leverage Award*	Award Based on Leveraged Funds	TOTAL
Wisconsin	446,897	*2,603,315*	*0.81%*	96,536	543,433
Wyoming	199,849	*115,433*	*0.04%*	4,280	204,129
Subtotal (50 states, DC and	***$27,072,250***	***$322,132,240***	***100.00%***	***$11,945,250***	***$39,017,500***
Insular areas[a]					
American Samoa	200,000				200,000
Guam	200,000				200,000
N. Mariana Islands	200,000				200,000
U.S. Virgin Islands	200,000				200,000
Subtotal (insular areas)	***$800,000***				***$800,000***
Set asides					
Tribal and migrant program					413,859
Technical Assistance/ other					1,457,389
TOTAL	**$27,872,250**	***$322,132,240***	***100%***	**$11,945,250**	**$41,688,748**

Source: Table prepared by the Congressional Research Service. Total final awards and allowable leveraged claims were estimated by CRS based on HHS information provided on the FRIENDS National Resource Center website (regarding leverage claim amounts) and final FY2008 allotment amounts.

a. Each of the insular areas is eligible to receive (and currently does receive) CBCAP funds under consolidated grant rules (45 C.F.R. 97). This permits them to use CBCAP funds for a range of service purposes and exempts them from specific CBCAP application requirements if they do not intend to use the funds under the CBCAP program authority. Insular areas receiving CBCAP funds under the consolidated grant rules are ineligible to receive leverage awards because they do not appoint a lead entity to leverage funds.

Research, Demonstration, and Other Activities

CAPTA authorizes support for a wide range of research, technical assistance, data collection, demonstration, and other activities related to the identification, prevention, and treatment of child abuse and neglect. Funding provided for these activities is typically awarded by HHS, on a competitive basis, via contract, grant, or cooperative agreement. As discussed in greater detail below, the statute requires HHS to undertake or support certain research, data collection, and technical assistance and it permits HHS to do certain other related activities.

CAPTA funding appropriated for these required or permitted purposes is provided under the CAPTA "discretionary activities" account in the annual appropriations act. That account received $41.8 million in the FY2009 appropriations act (P.L. 111-8), of which Congress—as part of the appropriations process—directed HHS to use $16.4 million for the following purposes: $13.5 million to continue support for a home visitation initiative begun in FY2008; $500,000 for a feasibility study on the creation, development, and maintenance of a national registry of substantiated child abuse cases; and $2.4 million for 12 specific projects or programs located in eight states.

Required Activities

Under CAPTA, HHS is required (directly or through competitive grants, contracts, or agreements) to support certain research and projects and provide technical assistance. These required activities are listed below, including, in some instances, a short discussion of how HHS is meeting or has met the requirement.

- ***Establish a national clearinghouse on child abuse*** after consulting with other relevant federal agencies and their heads and soliciting public comment. HHS currently funds the Child Welfare Information Gateway (www.childwelfare.gov), which incorporates the former National Clearinghouse on Child Abuse and Neglect Information. The Child Welfare Information Gateway website offers a wide range of policy and practice resources regarding identifying, reporting, responding to, and treating child abuse and neglect.
- ***Collect and disseminate information related to child abuse and neglect identification, prevention, and treatment.*** Specifically, HHS must maintain, collect, and/or disseminate information on 1) programs related to the prevention, assessment, identification, and treatment of child abuse and neglect that are effective or promising and have the potential for broad implementation; 2) best practices for improving child protective systems; 3) best practices for addressing or making appropriate referrals related to the physical, developmental, and mental health needs of abused and neglected children; 4) the

incidence of child abuse and neglect in the United States, including, specifically, among populations determined as underserved and among cases related to alcohol or drug abuse; and 5) training resources available at the state and local level for individuals who engage in preventing, identifying, and treating child abuse and neglect. In addition to the Child Welfare Information Gateway, HHS funds a number of national resource centers and quality improvement centers that respond to these requirements.[90] For example, it currently supports the National Quality Improvement Center on Differential Response in Child Protective Services, and the National Center on Substance Abuse and Child Welfare.[91]

- ***Establish a national child abuse and neglect data collection and analysis system.*** The 1988 CAPTA amendments (P.L. 100-294) that added this requirement specified that the system must, to the extent practicable, coordinate existing federal, state, regional, and local child welfare data systems; include state-reported data on the number of deaths due to child abuse and neglect; and include standardized state-reported information on false, unfounded, unsubstantiated, and substantiated reports of child abuse or neglect. Further, it required HHS to compile and make available the state-reported child abuse and neglect data. HHS has established the National Child Abuse and Neglect Data System (NCANDS) and produces an annual publication (*Child Maltreatment*) that compiles and analyzes child abuse and neglect data reported by states. All states have submitted data to NCANDS on an annual basis, although this reporting is considered voluntary for states. Data collected via NCANDS may also be accessed by researchers for additional study through the HHS-funded National Data Archive on Child Abuse and Neglect housed at Cornell University.[92]
- ***Provide technical assistance to state and local public and private agencies and community-based organizations,*** including disability organizations and people who work with children with disabilities. The purpose of the technical assistance is to aid these agencies and organizations in developing, improving, and carrying out programs related to prevention, assessment, identification, and treatment of child abuse and neglect and in replicating successful programs. HHS funds the National Resource Center on Child Protective Services, among other relevant resource centers and projects (including some of

those also charged with collecting and disseminating relevant information).

- ***Support an ongoing research program designed to provide information on how to better protect children from abuse or neglect and to improve the well-being of abused or neglected children.*** The research program must be interdisciplinary, and include some field-initiated research projects as well as longitudinal research. HHS must compile, analyze, and publish a summary of the research funded under the program. Further, HHS is required to establish priorities for this research program, solicit public comment on those priorities, and maintain an official record of the comment. HHS makes annual competitive grant announcements for child abuse and neglect related research and has published a notice of research priorities in the *Federal Register.*[93]

  The statute includes a list of topics on which HHS may choose to focus its required research topics, including the 1) nature and scope of child abuse and neglect and its causes, prevention, assessment, identification, treatment, cultural and socio-economic distinctions, and consequences;• 2) effects of abuse and neglect on a child's development and successful early intervention or other services needed; 3) appropriate, effective, and culturally sensitive investigative, administrative, and judicial systems with respect to child abuse cases (including multi-disciplinary and coordinated decision-making procedures); 4) evaluation and dissemination of best practices to improve child protective services systems; 5) effective interagency collaboration between child protective services and the juvenile justice system to improve delivery and continuity of services; 6) evaluation of redundancies and gaps in services to prevent child abuse and neglect to enable better use of resources; 7) nature, scope, and practice of voluntary relinquishment to foster care or state guardianship for the purpose of receiving health or mental health services for low-income children; and 8) information on the national incidence of child abuse and neglect.

- ***Survey the national incidence of child abuse and neglect and report findings to Congress.*** The Keeping Children and Families Safe Act of 2003 (P.L. 108-36) required HHS to conduct a fourth national incidence survey of child abuse and neglect (NIS-4) and to report back to Congress by July 2007.[94] Specifically, Congress asked HHS to look at and report on the 1) incidence and prevalence of child maltreatment by an array of demographic characteristics (e.g., age, sex, race, family structure, household relationship, school enrollment and education attainment, disability, grandparents as caregivers, labor force status, work status, and income status); 2) any increase or decrease in the number and severity of child abuse cases; 3) incidence of reported child abuse cases that are substantiated and unsubstantiated; 4) number of substantiated cases that result in a judicial finding of child abuse or neglect or related criminal court convictions; 5) extent to which the number of reports of child abuse or neglect that are not substantiated or are false interferes with a state's ability to respond to serious cases of child abuse and neglect; 6) extent to which lack of resources or adequate training for mandatory reporters contribute to a state's inability to respond to serious cases of child abuse or neglect; 7) number of unsubstantiated, false, or unfounded reports that result in a child's out-of-home placement and the length of that placement; 8) extent to which unsubstantiated reports return as more serious cases of child abuse or neglect; 9) incidence and prevalence of physical, sexual, and emotional abuse and physical and emotional neglect in foster care; and 10) incidence and outcomes of abuse allegations reported within the context of divorce, custody, or other family court proceedings, and the interaction between the court and the child protective services system. Survey data were collected from 2005 to 2007, but as of early November 2009, the report to Congress on this research has not yet been made available.[95]

- ***Establish a peer review process for awarding certain grants or contracts.*** The peer review process spelled out in statute is designed to ensure consultation with experts in the field in making grants under the CAPTA research program and to enhance the quality and usefulness of the research. In addition, for certain grants or projects funded via CAPTA, the statute requires evaluations to assess their effectiveness.

Permitted Activities

Permitted activities for HHS include establishing an Office of Child Abuse and Neglect, establishing an Advisory Board on Child Abuse and Neglect, and supporting research or demonstration projects and programs on specific topics listed in the statute that are related to the prevention of child abuse and neglect. These and other permitted activities are described below.

- ***Establish an Office of Child Abuse and Neglect.*** HHS has established the Office of Child Abuse and Neglect (OCAN) within the Children's Bureau. As stipulated in law, the purposes of the office are to carry out and coordinate the functions and activities of CAPTA, to ensure the necessary expertise and intradepartmental coordination whenever it is necessary to do this, and to ensure regular intradepartmental and interdepartmental consultation with all agencies involved in child abuse and neglect activities.[96] The Federal Interagency Working Group on Child Abuse and Neglect, with representation from more than 40 federal agencies, meets in-person on a quarterly basis, and some members are in more frequent contact by conference call. The purposes of the working group include providing a forum through which staff from relevant federal agencies can communicate and exchange ideas concerning child abuse and neglect related programs and activities and providing a basis for collective action through which funding and resources can be maximized.[97]
- ***Appoint an Advisory Board on Child Abuse and Neglect.*** HHS is permitted to establish an Advisory Board on Child Abuse and Neglect to make recommendations concerning specific child abuse and neglect related issues to the agency and Congress. The current law stipulates certain necessary characteristics and qualifications for members appointed to this board.[98] Under prior law, HHS was required to appoint an Advisory Board on Child Abuse and Neglect, and during the first half of the 1990s—when the last Board was appointed—it released several reports.[99] Those reports made specific recommendations related to responding to abuse or neglect, preventing abuse and neglect (including through implementation of universal voluntary neonatal home visiting and creation of comprehensive neighborhood-based prevention strategies), and prevention of child abuse and neglect related fatalities (including through increased knowledge of the problem, a primary focus on "safety" in all child and family programs, interdisciplinary and other efforts to improve investigation and prosecution of child abuse and neglect related fatalities, and improved family preservation and family support services).[100]
- ***Support additional research or fund other activities related to the prevention and treatment of child abuse and neglect.*** In addition to the required research program, the statute gives HHS authority to fund a range of research or other activities intended to advance cross-

> agency and cross-discipline links in ways that are expected to improve how CPS responds to and serves children and families. These include projects that encourage linkages across child welfare, law, education, health, mental health, and law enforcement agencies, as well as across public and private agencies, including faith-based and community-based groups. The act specifically suggests collaboration efforts to improve school-based prevention, identification, and assessment of child abuse and neglect; "triage" procedures in screening and responding to reports of child abuse and neglect; recognition of substance abuse or domestic violence in neglect situations; and better health evaluations and forensic diagnosis of abuse or neglect.

Many projects related to improving training or practice for CPS workers and related personnel are listed in the statute. HHS may choose to make grants to, or contracts with, states, public and private agencies or organizations, or a combination of those entities to improve the training of supervisory and non-supervisory child welfare workers, and for training of child protective services workers regarding, specifically, best practices in working with families from initial contact through the completion of an investigation and concerning their legal duties and responsibilities related to protecting the legal rights of children and families. In addition, HHS may provide grants to support development of risk and safety assessment tools for child protective service workers; training for mandated child abuse and neglect reporters; and improvement in the recruitment, selection, and training of volunteers in public or private child, youth, and family service organizations to prevent child abuse and neglect.

Finally, HHS is explicitly permitted to make grants or enter into contracts with various entities that provide additional supports to, among other activities, 1) establish and operate safe and family-friendly locations for court-ordered and supervised visitation between children and abusing parents and to facilitate the exchange of children for visits with noncustodial parents in domestic violence cases; 2) develop procedures for safe placement of children with kin; 3) establish or maintain a network of mutual parent support and self-help programs; 4) support respite and crisis nursery programs; 5) provide hospital-based information and referral services to parents of children with disabilities, parents of children who have been abused or neglected, and their children; and 6) support other innovative and promising programs related to preventing and treating child abuse and neglect.

The Children's Bureau typically awards grants, contracts, or cooperative agreements for its required and permitted activities near the end of the fiscal year and a list of awardees can be viewed online.[101]

Set Asides and Earmarks in the Appropriations Process

The CAPTA "discretionary activities" account has frequently been used to fund certain set-asides and/or earmarks as directed by Congress through the appropriations process. Typically, these directives are given in the conference report or other explanatory statement accompanying the final enacted annual appropriations act and may respond to specific Administration or individual lawmaker requests, or to broader congressional concerns.

Home Visitation

For example, Congress used the appropriations process in FY2008 and FY2009 to respond to a request by the Bush Administration for additional CAPTA discretionary activities funds to support a home visitation initiative. The Bush Administration requested (and received) $10 million for this purpose for FY2008, and used the funding to launch the Supporting Evidence-Based Home Visitation Programs to Prevent Child Abuse and Neglect initiative.[102] For FY2009, Congress provided $13.5 million to continue this initiative. The FY2010 budget request from the Obama Administration seeks continued funding for this initiative as well as funding for a separate and new program of grants to states to support home visitation programs for families with young children and those expecting children.[103]

Feasibility of a National Child Abuse Registry

Also as part of the FY2009 appropriations process, Congress provided that $500,000 of the CAPTA discretionary activities funding be made available to fund a feasibility study related to a national registry of substantiated child abuse. Congress required such a study in 2006 legislation (the Adam Walsh Child Protection and Safety Act, P.L. 109-248, Section 633) but had not provided discrete funding for the project before the FY2009 appropriations legislation (P.L. 111-8). Prior to this funding becoming available, HHS used general departmental funds to begin a feasibility study and it issued an interim report in early 2009. That report cited a number of barriers to implementation and had four main conclusions:

- potential benefits of a national child abuse and neglect registry are largely unknown and no data are available to quantify them;

- the statute provides for voluntary participation by states, and this could result in a registry that includes little information and fails to fulfill its intent;
- the statute does not permit inclusion in the registry of sufficient information to accurately identify perpetrators (information is limited to an individual's name, and because many names are common, this would result in many misidentified "perpetrators"); and
- the intent of the registry needs to be clarified (is it for child abuse and neglect investigative purposes only or may it also be used for background checks related to employment or licensing?).

The report also summarizes some issues related to "due process" that the creation of a national registry of substantiated child abuse and neglect would raise. These include differences in the level of evidence used to make decisions to substantiate a report of child abuse or neglect; the strength of hearing or appeal procedures in place locally to challenge those decisions; whether individuals included in the registry must be notified that they are included; and the implications of being included on such a registry. It asserts that "there can be no federal substitute for procedural protections at the state or local level" and, further, that "HHS believes the only feasible way to effectively and efficiently provide due process protections is to require that submitting jurisdictions certify that for cases submitted to the national registry, minimum due process protections were available to the perpetrator." [104]

HHS has awarded the $500,000 for the final study to Walter R. McDonald and Associates (and subcontractor ABA Center on Children and the Law) to continue work on this issue, including studying 1) how common it is for perpetrators to be listed in multiple states' child abuse registries; 2) states' interest in and concerns about participating in a national registry; 3) the data systems containing current state registries; and 4) legal issues involved and the adequacy of states' due process procedures.

Individual Requests

Finally, Congress has also frequently used the CAPTA discretionary activities account to fund specific projects in specific locations at the request of individual lawmakers. For FY2008, it directed $1.8 million to support eight projects in eight states, and for FY2009, it directed $2.4 million to support 12 projects in nine states.[105]

Children's Justice Act Grants

Grants for states to make improvements to the investigation, prosecution, and overall handling of child abuse and neglect cases are authorized under Section 107 of CAPTA. These grants are commonly referred to as "Children's Justice Act grants" because they were originally enacted as part of a 1986 law, the Children's Justice Act (Title I of P.L. 99-401). Funding for the grants is provided as an annual set-aside from the Crime Victims Fund (and is not appropriated out of the general treasury).[106] The maximum annual set-aside for this purpose is $20 million. Of that amount, $17 million was made available for FY2009 for grants to all eligible states, including the District of Columbia, Puerto Rico, and the four territories (Guam, American Samoa, the Northern Mariana Islands, and the U.S. Virgin Islands) and $3 million was reserved for use by tribes. Funding provided to the states and territories is administered by HHS. Funds reserved for the tribes are administered by the Department of Justice.

Use of Funds

The purposes of these funds are to 1) improve the handling of child abuse and neglect cases, especially those involving child sexual abuse and exploitation, in a manner that limits additional trauma to the child victims; 2) improve the investigation and prosecution of child abuse and neglect cases, especially those involving child sexual abuse and exploitation; and 3) improve the handling of cases of suspected child abuse or neglect related fatalities, as well as those involving child maltreatment victims with disabilities and child maltreatment victims with serious health-related problems.

States must use funds received under this grant to establish a multi-disciplinary taskforce to review and evaluate state investigative, administrative, and judicial handling of child abuse and neglect cases. The task force must include professionals with knowledge and experience related to the criminal justice system and issues of child maltreatment, including court personnel (judges, attorneys, children's attorneys, and court-appointed special advocates), representatives of law enforcement, CPS agencies, and parents' groups; health and mental health professionals; parents; and individuals experienced in working with children with disabilities. The taskforce must review and evaluate state investigative, administrative, and civil and criminal judicial handling of cases of child abuse and neglect, and make certain policy and training recommendations to improve those processes.

Under HHS guidance, states are not permitted to use Children's Justice Act grants for child abuse prevention programs or treatment services but must use them to support system improvements.[107] In addition to supporting the administration and work of the taskforce, states also use Children's Justice Act grants to hold multi-disciplinary conferences; provide training and cross-training on relevant topics (e.g., forensic interviewing) or for certain individuals (e.g., mandatory reporters of child abuse or neglect, court appointed special advocates, and guardians ad litem); support administration of or provide training related to Children's Advocacy Centers; permit co-location of staff (e.g., a social worker in police station); fund time-limited demonstrations of model initiatives or programs; buy certain equipment (e.g., digital cameras); and build certain facilities (e.g. family-friendly environments for interviewing).[108]

Eligibility Requirements

To be eligible to apply for Children's Justice Act grants, a state must meet all the eligibility requirements for CAPTA state grants (see "Requirements for Receipt of State Grant Funds"); establish a multi-disciplinary task force to study state administrative, judicial, and investigative practice related to child abuse and neglect cases (as described in "Use of Funds"); receive recommendations from the task force in the initial year grants are funded (and every three years thereafter) and implement those recommendations (or an alternative plan that meets the purpose of the recommendation, as determined by HHS); and annually submit an application and performance report to HHS.[109]

Table 4. Estimated FY2009 Children's Justice Act Awards, By State.

State	Estimated FY2009 Award
Alabama	$271,596
Alaska	$85,939
Arizona	$379,349
Arkansas	$188,167
California	$1,900,799
Colorado	$285,233
Connecticut	$211,772
Delaware	$90,560
District of Columbia	$72,429

Table 4. (Continued)

State	Estimated FY2009 Award
Florida	$847,515
Georgia	$549,311
Hawaii	$106,348
Idaho	$130,413
Illinois	$680,973
Indiana	$362,910
Iowa	$190,311
Kansas	$187,289
Kentucky	$248,014
Louisiana	$262,923
Maine	$105,120
Maryland	$317,997
Massachusetts	$332,603
Michigan	$532,595
Minnesota	$298,566
Mississippi	$201,612
Missouri	$331,020
Montana	$93,292
Nebraska	$137,994
Nevada	$180,173
New Hampshire	$108,811
New Jersey	$457,043
New Mexico	$148,670
New York	$920,461
North Carolina	$487,395
North Dakota	$78,166
Ohio	$592,754
Oklahoma	$227,411
Oregon	$220,192
Pennsylvania	$0[a]
Puerto Rico	$247,811
Rhode Island	$95,977
South Carolina	$259,048
South Dakota	$88,833
Tennessee	$340,222

Table 4. (Continued)

State	Estimated FY2009 Award
Texas	$1,356,332
Utah	$211,102
Vermont	$75,907
Virginia	$410,179
Washington	$353,019
West Virginia	$126,403
Wisconsin	$310,597
Wyoming	$74,726
Subtotal—50 States, District of Columbia and Puerto Rico	***$16,773,884***
Insular Areas *(consolidated grants)*	
American Samoa	$55,037
Guam	$60,819
Northern Mariana Islands	$53,497
U.S. Virgin Islands	$56,763
Subtotal - Insular areas	***$226,116***
Tribal program	*$3,000,000*
TOTAL	**$20,000,000**

Source: Table prepared by Congressional Research Service.

Note: Estimates exclude an award amount for Pennsylvania because that state did not apply for these funds for FY2009. Estimates are based on a $50,000 allotment to every remaining state and territory with the remainder distributed to those same jurisdictions based on the relative share of child population in each state (2007 Census Bureau estimates).

a. Pennsylvania did not apply for FY2009 funding under this grant program.

Distribution of Funds

For FY2009, 49 states, the District of Columbia, and Puerto Rico were expected to receive Children's Justice Act funds (Pennsylvania did not submit an application). In addition, each of the four insular areas were expected to receive funding: American Samoa, Guam, the Northern Mariana Islands, and the U.S. Virgin Islands. The statute authorizes HHS to make grants to states but does not provide a formula or method to do this. HHS distributes the funds to states in the same manner that funds are allocated for CAPTA state grants: all eligible states that apply for the funds receive a base grant of $50,000 and the remaining funds are distributed to each of those states based on their relative share of the child (under age 18) population. Table 4 shows expected

FY2009 distribution of funds. Because Pennsylvania did not apply for the grants, funding that would otherwise go to it is reallocated and distributed among those states that did apply.

FUNDING AUTHORIZED AND APPROPRIATED UNDER CAPTA

The final section of this report discusses funding authorized by CAPTA and includes a table showing a history of funding appropriated under that authority (beginning with FY1992). CAPTA does not include *funding* authority for the state grants for programs relating to the investigation and prosecution of child abuse and neglect cases. As noted above, these grants, commonly referred to as Children's Justice Act grants, are authorized in Section 107 of CAPTA. However, they are funded under an annual set-aside (maximum of $20 million) from the Crime Victims Fund.[110] This section of the report does not include further discussion of those grants or their funding. Instead, the funding authorization levels and appropriations described below relate only to the grants and other activities for which *funding* authority is provided in CAPTA and for which funds must be appropriated out of the general treasury.

CAPTA contains *two* separate funding authorizations, one for grants and activities under Title I (i.e., state grants and discretionary activities) and another for grants under Title II (community-based grants). Traditionally, Congress appropriates funding under these *two* funding authorizations in *three* separate accounts. As shown in Table 5, actual appropriations typically fall below the authorized funding level.

Title I Funding Authorization

Section 112 of CAPTA provides a "general" Title I funding authorization level, which was set at $120 million for FY2004 and at "such sums as may be necessary" for each of FY2005-FY2008. This funding authority is currently expired but Congress appropriated $68.3 million in funds to meet Title I CAPTA purposes for FY2009 (P.L. 111-8), and legislation pending in Congress (H.R. 3293) would appropriate a similar amount for FY2010.

Table 5. Funding Authorized and Appropriated Under CAPTA, FY1992-FY2009 "Such Sums" Refers to a Statutory Funding Authorization of "Such Sums as May be Necessary" (dollars shown in millions)

Fiscal Year	TITLE I				TITLE II		TOTAL CAPTA	
	Funding Authorized	Funding Appropriated						
		State Grants	Discretionary Activities	Subtotal	Funding Authorized	Funding Appropriated	Funding Authorized	Funding Appropriated
1992	$100.0	$20.5	$14.6	$35.2	$45.0	$5.4	$145.0	$40.5
1993	such sums	$20.4	$16.2	$36.6	such sums	$5.3	such sums	$41.9
1994	such sums	$22.9	$15.9	$38.8	such sums	$5.3	such sums	$44.1
1995	such sums	$22.9	$15.4	$38.3	such sums	$31.4[a]	such sums	$69.7
1996	$100.0	$21.0	$14.2	$35.2	$66.0	$23.0	$166.0	$58.2
1997	such sums	$21.0	$14.2	$35.2	such sums	$32.8	such sums	$68.0
1998	such sums	$21.0	$14.1	$35.1	such sums	$32.8	such sums	$67.9
1999	such sums	$21.0	$14.1	$35.2	such sums	$32.8	such sums	$68.0
2000	such sums	$21.0	$18.0	$39.1	such sums	$32.8	such sums	$71.9
2001	such sums	$21.0	$33.2[b]	$54.2	such sums	$32.8	such sums	$87.1
2002	expired	$22.0	$26.1	$48.1	expired	$33.4	expired	$81.5
2003	expired	$21.9	$33.8	$55.7	expired	$33.2	expired	$88.9
2004	$120.0	$21.9	$34.4	$56.3	$80.0	$33.2	$200.0	$89.5
2005	such sums	$27.3	$31.6	$58.9	such sums	$42.9	such sums	$101.8
2006	such sums	$27.0	$25.4	$52.5	such sums	$42.4	such sums	$94.9
2007	such sums	$27.0	$25.8	$52.8	such sums	$42.4	such sums	$95.2
2008	such sums	$26.5	$37.1[c]	$63.7	such sums	$41.7	such sums	$105.4
2009	expired	$26.5	$41.8[c]	$68.3	expired	$41.7	expired	$110.0

Source: Table prepared by the Congressional Research Service. Parts may not sum to total due to rounding.

Note: The table does not include any funds provided for Children's Justice Act grants. The program authority for these grants is included in Section 107 (Title I) of CAPTA. However, funding is not authorized for these grants under CAPTA and they are not funded out of the general treasury. Instead, funds are reserved for these grants out of the Crime Victims Fund, as authorized by the Victims of Crime Act. (As of FY2001, the set-aside is up to $20 million annually.)

a. Funding increased due to consolidation of CAPTA Title II funding with other categorical prevention programs.

b. Funding increase appears to be related to earmark projects added to this account in report language accompanying the appropriations act. Earmarks have been included on this account in most subsequent fiscal years, with the notable exceptions of FY2006 and FY2007.

c. FY2008 funding includes $10 million for home visitation initiative; FY2009 funding includes $13.5 million for that home visitation initiative and $500,000 for a feasibility study related to standards for a national registry of substantiated child abuse and neglect.

Section 112 further adds that out of the total funding provided for Title I (under the general authorization of funding), HHS must make 30% available for "discretionary activities" provided for in Title I of CAPTA. In practice, however, Congress regularly overrides this statutory language by appropriating CAPTA Title I funds in two separate accounts, one for "Child Abuse State Grants" and a separate one for "Child Abuse Discretionary Activities." The latter supports research, technical assistance, and other activities required or authorized under Title I of CAPTA , along with (in most years) some projects that are consistent with CAPTA purposes and are specified during that appropriations process.[111] Funding provided for "discretionary activities" has ranged from roughly 40% to 60% of overall Title I funding. For FY2009, funds appropriated for CAPTA's "discretionary activities" account totaled 61% of the overall Title I funding.

Title II Funding Authorization

Section 210 of CAPTA authorizes funding for Title II community-based grants to prevent child abuse and neglect. The funding authorization level for these grants was set at $80 million for FY2004 and at such sums as may be necessary for FY2005-FY2008. This funding authority is currently expired but Congress nonetheless appropriated $41.7 million for FY2009 (P.L. 111-8), and FY2010 appropriations legislation pending in Congress (H.R. 3293) would appropriate that same amount for FY2010.

Appendix A. Scope of State Child Protective Services Work

Data in Table A-1 are provided to suggest the scope of activity by state protective services that is related to the CAPTA directive that states have procedures to receive and respond to allegations of child abuse and neglect. The population data shown are the Census Bureau estimate of the number of children (individuals under age 18) living in each state on July 1, 2007. The FY2007 program data include the number of allegations of child abuse or neglect (referrals) received by CPS, the number of those referrals that were investigated (reports), and the number and rate of children found to be victims of abuse or neglect. The victim rate refers to the number of children who were reported to be victims of child maltreatment for every 1,000 children in the population.

Table A-1. Child Population and Number of Child Abuse or Neglect Referrals, Investigations, and Victims Reported by States, FY2007 A Blank Cell Indicates that State Did Not Report Usable Data on the Given Topic for FY2007

State	Child Population (2007)	Allegations of Child Abuse or Neglect (Referrals)	Allegations that Received a CPS Investigation (Reports)	Victims	
				Number	*Rate*[a]
Alabama	1,123,537	30,462	18,710	9,247	8.2
Alaska	182,218	9,775	4,906	3,138	17.2
Arizona	1,669,866	33,433	33,188	4,025	2.4
Arkansas	700,537	40,184	27,846	9,847	14.1
California	9,383,924	339,303	232,297	88,319	9.4
Colorado	1,192,679	65,826	31,520	10,588	8.9
Connecticut	820,216		26,479	9,875	12.0
Delaware	205,646	7,306	5,693	2,116	10.3
District of Columbia	113,720	4,888	4,506	2,757	24.2
Florida	4,043,560	259,864	154,951	53,484	13.2

Table A-1. (Continued)

State	Child Population (2007)	Allegations of Child Abuse or Neglect (Referrals)	Allegations that Received a CPS Investigation (Reports)	Victims	
				Number	*Rate*[a]
Georgia	2,531,609	63,621	48,965	35,729	14.1
Hawaii	285,694		2,527	2,075	7.3
Idaho	407,712		7,089	1,582	3.9
Illinois	3,199,159		68,101	31,058	9.7
Indiana	1,586,518	68,971	41,900	18,380	11.6
Iowa	711,403	39,847	23,093	14,051	19.8
Kansas	696,082	31,402	16,912	2,272	3.3
Kentucky	1,003,973	63,612	48,600	18,778	18.7
Louisiana	1,079,560		19,293	9,468	8.8
Maine	279,467	16,678	6,710	4,118	14.7
Maryland	1,358,797				
Massachusetts	1,432,856	67,793	39,801	37,690	26.3
Michigan	2,446,856				
Minnesota	1,260,282	56,581	18,993	6,847	5.4
Mississippi	768,704	26,964	17,871	7,002	9.1
Missouri	1,424,830	102,579	54,635	7,235	5.1
Montana	219,498	12,852	8,699	1,886	8.6
Nebraska	446,145	23,050	11,290	4,108	9.2
Nevada	660,002	22,492	16,342	5,417	8.2
New Hampshire	298,186	16,350	6,834	912	3.1
New Jersey	2,063,789		44,606	7,543	3.7
New Mexico	500,276	30,130	14,853	6,065	12.1
New York	4,413,414		155,509	83,502	18.9
North Carolina	2,217,680		66,814	25,976	11.7
North Dakota	142,809		3,586	1,288	9.0
Ohio	2,751,874		77,436	38,484	14.0
Oklahoma	899,507	62,965	35,873	13,179	14.7
Oregon	862,908	63,504	26,381	11,552	13.4
Pennsylvania	2,786,719		23,513	4,177	1.5
Puerto Rico	1,002,944		15,709	10,696	10.7

Table A-1. (Continued)

State	Child Population (2007)	Allegations of Child Abuse or Neglect (Referrals)	Allegations that Received a CPS Investigation (Reports)	Victims	
				Number	*Rate*[a]
Rhode Island	233,115	12,443	7,710	3,857	16.5
South Carolina	1,059,917	27,293	18,337	12,762	12.0
South Dakota	196,890	14,481	3,627	1,485	7.5
Tennessee	1,471,486		62,183	16,059	10.9
Texas	6,623,366	202,015	166,584	71,111	10.7
Utah	816,822	32,424	20,386	13,611	16.7
Vermont	131,353	12,327	2,564	872	6.6
Virginia	1,826,179	58,060	30,196	6,413	3.5
Washington	1,536,368	74,381	35,262	6,984	4.5
West Virginia	387,381	31,813	21,962	7,109	18.4
Wisconsin	1,321,279	54,704	26,978	7,856	5.9
Wyoming	125,365	5,070	2,442	772	6.2
National estimate[b]	**74,904,677**	**3,220,000**	**2,040,000**	**794,000**	**10.6**

Source: Table prepared by the Congressional Research Service based on U.S. Census Bureau population estimates for 2007 and data included in HHS, *Child Maltreatment 2007* (April 2009).

a. Victim rate refers to the number of children who were reported to be victims of child maltreatment for every 1,000 children in the population.

b. Not all states reported data in each category. National estimates for referrals, reports, and victims are from *Child Maltreatment 2007* and derived by HHS based on average number of referrals, reports, or victims provided among all states that did report data. The total number of referrals reported was 2,085,443; of investigations, 1,860,262, and of victims, 753,357.

Referrals and investigations typically involve more than one child. For example, on a national basis, states received 3.2 million referrals during FY2007 that alleged abuse or neglect related to an estimated 5.8 million children. CPS workers responded with an investigation, or some other assessment of the family, for 1.9 million of the referrals, and the estimated number of children involved in those investigations (or assessments) was approximately 3.5 million. Finally, the table shows the number and rate of children found to be victims in each state.

APPENDIX B. CHILD, FAMILY, AND CAREGIVER RISK FACTORS AMONG CHILDREN IN FAMILIES INVESTIGATED FOR CHILD ABUSE OR NEGLECT

The National Survey of Child and Adolescent Well-Being (NSCAW), required by Congress under Section 429 of the Social Security Act, included a nationally representative sample of children in families investigated for abuse or neglect . Table B-1 shows selected developmental and other risk factors among those children compared to children in the general population. Findings refer to children in families investigated for child abuse or neglect, as a whole, and without regard to whether an abuse or neglect finding was substantiated by the CPS investigator.

Table B-1. Selected Developmental and Other Risk Factors for Children

Among preschool aged children[a], risk for poor scores on standardized measures related to:	Children in families investigated for abuse or neglect	Children in the general population
Neurological development or impairment	53%	14%
Cognitive development	31%	2.5%
Language skills development	14%	2.5%
Problem behavior	27%	17%
Among school age children[a], percentage at risk for poor scores on standardized measures related to:		
Verbal and non-verbal intelligence scores	5%	2%
Reading achievement	5%	2%
Math achievement	12%	2.5%
Problem behavior (caregiver assessment)[b]	45%	17%
Social skills	38%	16%
Living skills	10%	2.5%
Depression	15%	9%

Source: Table prepared by Congressional Research Service based on NSCAW Research Brief 3 (undated). For children in families investigated for abuse or neglect, findings are based on survey data collected in 1999-2000.

a. Specific pre-school or school age groups studied varied by measure used but the share of general population children, that is, the "normative sample," was based on a comparable age group in each case.

b. Thirty-six percent of the youth in investigated families (ages 11-15) gave reports of their own behavior that indicated clinical or borderline problem behavior.

Table B-2. Families Where a Child Abuse or Neglect Investigation Occurred By Presence of Certain Risk Factors and Post-investigation Service Level As assessed by the CPS investigative caseworker

Family/Caregiver Risk Factors	All Families Subject to an Investigation	Post-investigation Service Level		
		Families Receiving No Services	*Families Receiving In-Home Services*	*Families Where Child Was Placed Out of the Home*
Prior report of maltreatment	51%	46%	57%	66%
Trouble paying for basic necessities	24%	16%	34%	47%
High stress in family	52%	43%	66%	73%
Low social support	31%	24%	39%	53%
Only one supportive caregiver in the family	54%	52%	54%	67%
Poor parenting skills	33%	20%	47%	79%
Unrealistic expectations of child	17%	9%	28%	44%
Excessive/inappropriate discipline	8%	5%	13%	19%
Serious mental health problem	15%	9%	22%	36%
Intellectual/cognitive impairment	7%	5%	9%	12%
Active drug abuse	9%	4%	12%	37%
Active alcohol abuse	8%	3%	13%	29%
Recent history of arrest	12%	8%	16%	34%
Active domestic violence (against primary caregiver)	13%	11%	15%	25%
History of domestic violence (against primary caregiver)	30%	25%	36%	44%
History of abuse or neglect (against primary caregiver)	22%	15%	32%	39%

Source: Table compiled by the Congressional Research Service based on data included in the National Survey of Child and Adolescent Well-Being, *CPS Sample Component, Wave 1 Data Analysis Report,* April 2005, Chapter 4.

Note: Proportions shown in the source document were weighted percentages, and in this report, they are additionally rounded to the nearest whole number.

Table B-2 presents NSCAW findings concerning family and caregiver risk factors among the families of all children investigated for abuse and neglect, as well as by the level of services received following the investigation. These findings are based on the initial wave of data collection in the survey which was fielded in 1999-2000.

APPENDIX C. TRENDS IN REPORTED CHILD ABUSE AND NEGLECT VICTIMS AND TYPES OF ABUSE OR NEGLECT EXPERIENCED

Table C-1 shows national estimates of children subject to an investigation for child abuse or neglect and those found to be victims of child abuse or neglect. Although these data were all reported under the National Child Abuse and Neglect Data Systems (NCANDS), the quality and kind of data reported varies significantly by year. In the earlier years, national estimates may necessarily have been derived based on information reported by a limited number of states. In more recent years, the quality of the data reported has improved and nearly all states reported these data. Therefore, estimates for more recent years may be more accurate than those for earlier years.

Table C-1. National Estimates of Children Who Were the Subject of Child Maltreatment Investigations and Those Found to Be Victims, 1990-2007 Rates shown refer to the number of children who were the subject of an investigation, or the number of child victims, as shown in the respective column heading, per 1,000 children in the population

Year	Child Population	Children Who Were Subject of an Investigation	Rate of Children Who Were the Subject of an Investigation	Children Found to Be Victims of Maltreatment	Rate of Child Maltreatment Victims
1990	64,163,000	2,316,000	36.1	860,000	13.4
1991	65,070,000	2,486,000	38.2	911,000	14.0
1992	66,074,000	2,722,000	41.2	998,000	15.1
1993	66,962,000	2,819,000	42.1	1,025,000	15.3

Table C-1. (Continued)

Year	Child Population	Children Who Were Subject of an Investigation	Rate of Children Who Were the Subject of an Investigation	Children Found to Be Victims of Maltreatment	Rate of Child Maltreatment Victims
1994	67,803,000	2,855,000	42.1	1,031,000	15.2
1995	68,437,000	2,888,000	42.2	1,006,000	14.7
1996	69,022,000	2,899,000	42.0	1,015,000	14.7
1997	69,528,000	2,913,000	41.9	953,000	13.7
1998	69,872,000	2,939,000	42.1	904,000	12.9
1999	70,199,000	2,878,000	41.0	828,000	11.8
2000	72,343,000	3,038,000	43.2	883,000	12.2
2001	72,604,000	3,136,000	43.9	905,000	12.5
2002	73,979,000	3,240,000	43.8	910,000	12.3
2003	74,079,000	3,430,000	46.3	904,000	12.2
2004	74,262,000	3,572,000	48.1	891,000	12.0
2005	74,463,000	3,597,000	48.3	900,000	12.1
2006	74,686,000	3,577,000	47.9	904,000	12.1
2007	74,905,000	3,536,000	47.2	794,000	10.6

Source: Table prepared by the Congressional Research Service based on data from National Child Abuse and Neglect Data System (NCANDS) as shown in Table 3-3, *Child Maltreatment 2004* (1990-2001), Table 3-2 *Child Maltreatment 2006* (for 2002), and *Child Maltreatment 2007* (for 2003-2007).

Notes: Estimates are for the 50 states and the District of Columbia through 200; beginning with 2002, they also include Puerto Rico. Data were reported for the calendar year through 2002, and for the fiscal year thereafter. Estimates are shown rounded to the nearest 1,000.

Table C-2 shows trends in the share of child maltreatment victims experiencing certain types of maltreatment. In every year before FY2007, children that experienced more than one type of maltreatment were included in each type of maltreatment. However, data for FY2007 are not comparable to data provided for earlier years because of a change in how this information was reported by HHS. For example, before FY2007, if a child experienced both sexual abuse and physical abuse, he or she would be represented in both maltreatment categories. Beginning with FY2007, HHS reported a category for children experiencing "multiple maltreatments" (two or more types of abuse or neglect) and every other category includes children that were reported as experiencing that type of maltreatment only.

Table C-2. Share of Children Reported as Experiencing Maltreatment, by Type

Year	Neglect[a]	Physical Abuse	Sexual Abuse	Psychological Maltreatment	Multiple Maltreatments	Other	Unknown/ Missing
2000	62.7%	19.4%	10.1%	7.7%	[See note]	16.6%	0.3%
2001	59.2%	18.6%	9.6%	6.8%	[See note]	19.5%	0.3%
2002	60.6%	18.6%	9.9%	6.5%	[See note]	18.9%	0.2%
2003	63.6%	18.4%	9.7%	6.4%	[See note]	14.9%	0.2%
2004	61.1%	17.1%	9.5%	7.1%	[See note]	14.4%	4.1%
2005	64.8%	16.6%	9.3%	7.1%	[See note]	14.3%	1.1%
2006	66.3%	16.0%	8.8%	6.6%	[See note]	15.1%	1.2%
2007	59.0%	10.8%	7.6%	4.2%	13.1%	4.2%	0.1%

Source: Table prepared by the Congressional Research Service based on NCANDS data as reported by states and provided by HHS.

Note: For FY2000 through FY2006, the sum of percentages equals more than 100 because children for whom more than one maltreatment type was reported were included in more than one maltreatment-type category. For FY2007, a single maltreatment type is reported for all children, except that children who were reported with more than one maltreatment type are included in the category "multiple maltreatments."

a. In this table, the category of "neglect" includes the subset of neglect reported as "medical neglect."

APPENDIX D. CHILDREN WHO RECEIVE POST-INVESTIGATION SERVICES

Table D-1 uses state reported data to estimate the number of children who received services following an investigation or assessment. Not all states reported these data; the estimates should therefore be treated as rough.

Table D-1. National Estimates of Children Served Following an Investigation of Child Abuse or Neglect To be counted, the removal or in-home service must have occurred within 90 days of the investigation

CHILDREN FOUND TO BE VICTIMS										
Year	All Child Victims	Removed to Foster Care		Served in Home		All Child Victims				
						Served		*Not Served*		
2002	910,000	172,000	18.9%	363,000	39.9%	535,000	58.8%	375,000	41.2%
2003	905,000	167,000	18.5%	358,000	39.6%	525,000	58.0%	380,000	42.0%
2004	892,000	170,000	19.0%	359,000	40.2%	528,000	59.2%	364,000	40.8%
2005	900,000	196,000	21.8%	346,000	38.4%	542,000	60.2%	358,000	39.8%
2006	905,000	195,000	21.5%	338,000	37.4%	533,000	58.9%	372,000	41.1%
2007	794,000	164,000	20.7%	333,000	41.9%	497,000	62.6%	297,000	37.4%
CHILDREN NOT FOUND TO BE VICTIMS									
Year	All "Non-Victims"	Removed to Foster Care		Served in Home		All "Non-Victims"			
						Served		*Not Served*	
2002	2,330,000	96,000	4.1%	620,000	26.6%	716,000	30.7%	1,615,000	69.3%
2003	2,521,000	104,000	4.1%	644,000	25.6%	748,000	29.7%	1,773,000	70.3%
2004	2,684,000	104,000	3.9%	739,000	27.5%	843,000	31.4%	1,841,000	68.6%
2005	2,694,000	121,000	4.5%	749,000	27.8%	816,000	32.3%	1,824,189	67.7%
2006	2,669,000	119,000	4.4%	690,000	25.9%	809,000	30.3%	1,860,075	69.7%
2007	2,742,000	104,000	3.8%	757,000	27.6%	861,000	31.4%	1,881,000	68.6%

Source: Table prepared by the Congressional Research Service based on NCANDS data reported by states and provided or published by HHS.

Note: Data were reported by states for the calendar year in 2002 but for the fiscal year thereafter. Not all states (defined to include the District of Columbia and Puerto Rico) reported these data. Therefore, the numbers shown represent national estimates made by CRS that are based on the share of children receiving post-investigation follow-up services in those states that did report these data.

End Notes

[1] John Stirling, Jr. and Lisa Amaya-Jackson, "Understanding the Behavioral and Emotional Consequences of Child Abuse," *Pediatrics,* vol. 122, No. 3, September 2008, p.p. 667-673. Bessel A. van der Kolk, James Hopper and Joseph Crozier, "Child Abuse in America: Prevalence and Consequences," *Journal of Aggression, Maltreatment, and Trauma,* 2001. National Survey of Child and Adolescent Well-Being (NSCAW), "Need for Early Intervention Services Among Infants and Toddlers in Child Welfare," Research Brief No. 8, undated. NSCAW, "Adolescents Involved with Child Welfare: A Transition to Adulthood," Research Brief No. 11, undated. NSCAW briefs are available at http://www.acf.hhs.gov/programs/opre/abuse_neglect/nscaw/#reports. Comparison groups used in these studies varied. For instance, the negative outcome may be more likely among child abuse and neglect victims when compared to the general population or when compared to a prospectively matched comparison group. In addition, the studies varied in how they defined/determined who experienced abuse or neglect. Further, some studies include in the group of "maltreated" children only those children for whom abuse or neglect was "substantiated", others include the larger group of children for whom abuse or neglect was investigated, and still others may rely on a self-report of childhood abuse or neglect.

[2] Earlier legislation amending and/or reauthorizing funding for CAPTA includes, P.L. 95-266 (1978); Title VI, Chapter 7 of P.L. 97-35 (1981); P.L. 98-457 (1984); P.L. 99-401 (1986); P.L. 100-294 (1988); P.L. 101-126 (1989); P.L. 102-295 (1992); and P.L. 104-235 (1996).

[3] Section 111(2) of CAPTA. See also Section 111(4) of CAPTA for a more extensive definition of "sexual abuse."

[4] In this report the terms "child maltreatment" and "child abuse and neglect" are used interchangeably.

[5] Child Welfare Information Gateway, "Definitions of Child Abuse and Neglect: Summary of State Laws," State Statutes Series, Current as of April 2007, http://www.childwelfare.gov /systemwide/laws_policies/statutes/defineall.pdf.

[6] Abuse or exploitation of children that is perpetrated by a "stranger" or someone who is not directly responsible for the child's care may be handled by law enforcement agencies as a criminal matter. For related information, see CRS Report RL34050, *Missing and Exploited Children: Background, Policies, and Issues*, by Adrienne L. Fernandes.

[7] U.S. Department of Health and Human Services (HHS), Administration for Children and Families, *Child Maltreatment 2007,* (April 2009), p. 29. (Hereinafter HHS, *Child Maltreatment 2007.*) http://www.acf.hhs.gov/programs/cb/pubs/cm07/. Data on the relationship of the perpetrator of child abuse or neglect to the victim was missing for about 10% of the victims reported by states.

[8] HHS, *Child Maltreatment 2007*, Table 5-3.

[9] Child Welfare Information Gateway, *Mandatory Reporters of Child Abuse and Neglect: Summary of State Laws*, January 2008 at http://www.childwelfare.gov/systemwide /laws_policies/statutes/mandaall.pdf .

[10] Child Welfare Information Gateway, *Cross-Reporting Among Responders to Child Abuse and Neglect: Summary of State Laws*, December 2007 at http://www.childwelfare.gov /systemwide/laws_policies/statutes/xreportingall.pdf .

[11] U.S. Department of Health and Human Services (HHS), Assistant Secretary for Planning and Evaluation (ASPE) and Administration for Children and Families (ACF) *National Study of Child Protective Services Systems and Reform Efforts: Summary Report,* May 2003, p. p.3-6. *Child Maltreatment 2007,* p. 5.

[12] HHS, *Child Maltreatment 2007*, Figure 2-1. Percentages may not sum to the total because of rounding. States reported "other" as the source for 9% of the investigated referrals, the source was unknown or missing in 7% of the cases. Additional investigated referrals were made by alleged victims (0.6%) and alleged perpetrators (0.1%).

[13] Westat, Inc., *Recent Trends in Local Child Protective Services Practices,* prepared for HHS, ASPE, July 2009, pp. 10-19. Hereinafter, Westat, *Recent Trends in Local Child Protective Services Practices,* July 2009.

[14] Gila Shusterman, et al., *Alternative Responses to Child Maltreatment: Findings from NCANDS,* prepared for HHS, ASPE, July 2005, pp. 1-3; Lisa Merkel-Holguin, et al., *National Study on Differential Response in Child Welfare*, November 2006, pp. 10-11.

[15] Westat, *Recent Trends in Local Child Protective Services Practices,* July 2009, pp 1-3. This represents a significant decline from the 69% of local CPS agencies that indicated use of alternative response in a similar 2002 survey of CPS agencies. Researchers suggest the decrease may reflect a better understanding by local agencies of what an alternative response system is and thus a more accurate reporting of whether the local CPS actually has such a system. They note that among agencies indicating that they had an alternative response system, there was greater uniformity in practice.

[16] Ibid, 13-17.

[17] HHS, *Child Maltreatment 2007,* based on Table 3-1. The total number of state-reported victims in FY2007 was 753,357. However, two states, Maryland and Michigan, did not report the number of child abuse and neglect victims for FY2007. HHS derived the national estimate of 794,000 victims by applying the average victim rate in all reporting states to the child populations in Maryland and Michigan, adding that number to the reported child victims, and rounding to the nearest thousand.

[18] National Survey of Child and Adolescent Well-Being (NSCAW), *How Do Caseworker Judgments Predict Substantiation of Child Maltreatment,* Research Brief No. 6, undated.

[19] HHS, *Child Maltreatment 2007,* p.p. 125-159

[20] "Average" child maltreatment rate for each group of states was determined by comparing the child population in the given group of states to the number of victims in that same group of states.

[21] HHS, *Child Maltreatment 2007,* based on Table 3-1.

[22] Ibid.

[23] Ibid, p. 24.

[24] For example, see comments on data collection or reporting changes, made by some states for FY2007, including Florida, which no longer uses the category "indicated" in reporting child abuse and neglect case determinations (p. 130); Louisiana, which cites population displacement by Hurricane Katrina as a reason for lower numbers of investigations (p. 135-137); and New Jersey, which no longer reports "at-risk alternative response non-victim assessments" (p. 144).

[25] David Finkelhor. *Childhood Victimization: Violence, Crime, and Abuse in the Lives of Young People,* New York: Oxford University Press, 2008.

[26] Cited in John Fluke , Ying-Ying Yuan, et al., "Disproportionate Representation of Race and Ethnicity in Child Maltreatment: Investigation and Victimization," *Children and Youth Services* 25(2003)5/6: 359-374. A fourth NIS has recently been fielded but findings have not yet been made available.

[27] HHS, *Child Maltreatment,* 2007.

[28] See U.S. Department of Health and Human Services, *Children of Color in the Child Welfare System: Perspectives from the Child Welfare Community*, December 2003; Barbara Needall, et al., "Black Children in Foster Care and Placement in California," *Children and Youth Services Review* 25 (2003), pp. 393-408; A.M. Hines, et al., "Factors Related to Disproportionate Involvement of Children of Color in the Child Welfare System: A Review of Emerging Themes," *Children and Youth Services Review* 26 (2004), pp. 505-527; and Robert B. Hill, *Synthesis of Research on Disproportionality in Child Welfare: An Update,* Casey-CSSP Alliance for Racial Equity in the Child Welfare System, October 2006.

[29] Westat, *Recent Trends in Local Child Protective Services Practices,* July 2009, pp. 12-13. See also HHS, *Child Maltreatment 2007,* p. 79.

[30] Westat, *Recent Trends in Local Child Protective Services Practices,* July 2009, pp. 19-20.

[31] U.S. Department of Health and Human Services (HHS), Administration for Children and Families, *Child Maltreatment 2006,* (April 2008), pp. 85-87. http://www.acf.hhs.gov /programs/cb/pubs/cm06/.

[32] The National Survey of Child and Adolescent Well-Being (NSCAW) includes a nationally representative sample of children in families investigated for abuse or neglect. The initial survey was fielded in 1999-2000 and four follow-up "waves" of data collection (between 2001-2006) provided longitudinal data from the same families. Most of the findings discussed in this report are from the initial survey. More information on NSCAW and related research briefs are available on the website of the Office for Planning, Research and Evaluation (OPRE), Administration for Children and Families (ACF), HHS at http://www.acf.hhs.gov/programs/opre/abuse_neglect/nscaw/

[33] NSCAW, *CPS Sample Component Wave 1 Data Analysis Report*, April 2005, Chapter 4. (Hereinafter NSCAW, *CPS Sample, Wave 1*, April 2005.).

[34] Ibid, p. 4-15 – 4-22.

[35] NSCAW, *Children's Cognitive and Socioemotional Development and Their Receipt of Special Educational and Mental Health Services,* Research Brief No. 3, (undated).

[36] This requirement was added during the last reauthorization of CAPTA (P.L. 108-36, 2003). A companion provision was also included in the 2004 reauthorization of IDEA (P.L. 108-446).

[37] NSCAW, *Need for Early Intervention Services Among Infants and Toddlers in Child Welfare,* NSCAW Research Brief No. 8 (undated). The initial survey data were collected in 1999-2000. Following these same families over the next three years, researchers found that the share of children who qualified for special education services (under either Part C or Part B of IDEA depending on child's age) increased (at 18 and 36 months after the initial survey).

[38] Ibid.

[39] Based on funding levels, the largest federal child welfare programs are authorized under the Social Security Act, including the Title IV-E (Foster Care, Adoption Assistance, and Kinship Guardianship Assistance) programs and the Title IV-B (Child and Family Services) programs. For a brief description of all federal child welfare programs, see CRS Report RL34121, *Child Welfare: Recent and Proposed Federal Funding*, by Emilie Stoltzfus.

[40] Section 106(a) of CAPTA.

[41] Bracketed phrase is probable intent of the statute. Language is not specific. See Section 106(a)(6)(B) of CAPTA.

[42] Other territories that receive CAPTA state grant funds are American Samoa, Guam, the U.S. Virgin Islands, and the Northern Mariana Islands. Under P.L. 95-134 these jurisdictions (sometimes referred to as "insular areas") are permitted to submit a consolidated grant application to receive CAPTA grant funding along with funding under a range of other specified federal social services programs (see 45 C.F.R. 97). They do not need to meet specific requirements of a given program unless they intend to use the consolidated grant funding under the specific program authority. None of these jurisdictions is currently required to meet specific CAPTA requirements.

[43] As stated by HHS, a primary purpose of the CFSP is to "facilitate States' integration of the programs that serve children and families . . . into a continuum of services." The CFSP must include overall child and family services goals and, in addition to CAPTA state grants, must incorporate state plan and other requirements of the following programs authorized under the Social Security Act: Stephanie Tubbs Jones Child Welfare Services Program (Title IV-B, Subpart 1), Promoting Safe and Stable Families (Title IV-B, Subpart 2), and the Chafee Foster Care Independence Program, including Education and Training Vouchers (Section 477). In every year for which a five-year CFSP is not required, a state must submit an Annual Progress and Services Report (APSR) discussing progress made toward the CFSP goals and providing other updated information, including requests for funding for each of the programs. Failure of a state to meet requirements of any one of the programs included in the CFSP does not jeopardize its funding for other programs. The requirements of the five-

year CFSP are spelled out in federal regulation (45 CFR 1357.15) and in annual Program Instructions (for the most recent see ACYF-CB-PI-09-06, June 3, 2009 at http://www.acf.hhs.gov/programs/cb/laws_policies/policy/pi/2009/pi0906.pdf.

[44] For more information on both of these Title IV-B programs, see CRS Report RL33354, *The Promoting Safe and Stable Families Program: Reauthorization in the 109th Congress*, by Emilie Stoltzfus.

[45] Section 106(b)(1)(A) and (B), Section 106(b)(2) (matter proceeding subparagraph (A)), Section 106(b)(2)(C) and (D) of CAPTA. See CAPTA compilation at http://www.acf.hhs.gov/programs/cb/laws_policies/cblaws/capta03/index.htm.

[46] Section 106(b)(2)(A)(i) and Section 106(b)(2)(A)(iv) of CAPTA.

[47] Section 106(b)(2)(A)(ii) of CAPTA. The law further specifies that this notification does not necessarily mean CPS must make a finding of abuse or neglect (i.e., it does not constitute a federal definition of child abuse or neglect) nor does it require prosecution for any illegal action.

[48] Section 106(b)(2)(B)(i) and (ii) of CAPTA. Medical neglect cases must include instances of withholding of medically indicated treatment from disabled infants with life-threatening conditions.

[49] Section 106(b)(2)(a)(xv)(II) and Section 106(b)(2)(A) (xviii) of CAPTA.

[50] Section 106(b)(2)(A)(vii) of CAPTA.

[51] Section 106(b)(2(A)(v) and (vi) of CAPTA.

[52] Section 106(b)(2)(A)(xxi), Section 106(b)(2)(A)(iii), Section(b)(2)(B)(iii) and Section 113(b) of CAPTA.

[53] Section 106(b)(2)(A)(xii) of CAPTA.

[54] Section 106(b)(2)(A)(viii), (ix) and (x); Section 106(c)(5); and Section 106(b)(2)(B)(final sentence) of CAPTA. Referral of child "victims" for Part C services is limited to those children under age 3 for whom the investigation *substantiates* child abuse or neglect. See HHS, Children's Bureau, *Child Welfare Policy Manual,* Section 2.1A.1 http://www.acf.hhs.gov/j2ee/programs/cb/laws_policies/laws/cwpm/policy_dsp.jsp?citID=67.

[55] HHS, Children's Bureau, *Child Welfare Policy Manual,* Section 2.1A.1, Question 1.

[56] Section 106(c)(4)(B) of CAPTA.

[57] Section 106(b)(2)(A)(xii) of CAPTA.

[58] Section 106(b)(3) of CAPTA. The original construction of this provision (and probable current intent) applied it specifically to the confidentiality provisions that describe who may receive confidential access to records and when the public has access to information from those records. However, technical amendments are necessary to correct the cross-reference.

[59] Section 106(b)(2)(xix) and (xx) of CAPTA.

[60] Section 106(b)(2)(A)(xiv) and Section 106(c)(1)(A) of CAPTA. As of FY2009, 15 states (AK, DE, HI, ID, ME, MT, NE, NH, NM, ND, RI, SD, VT, WV, WY) and DC received the minimum allotment of funding distributed by population under Title II of CAPTA and were required to establish only one citizen review panel.

[61] Section 106(c)(2) through (6) of CAPTA.

[62] Section 106(b)(2)(a)(xv)(I), (xvi), and (xvii) of CAPTA. These CAPTA provisions were enacted in 1996 (P.L. 104-235). Similar provisions were enacted in Title IV-E of the Social Security Act as part of the Adoption and Safe Families Act (P.L. 105-89). See Section 471(a)(15)(D) and Section 475(5)(E) of the Social Security Act.

[63] Section 106(b)(2)(A)(xxii) of CAPTA. Title IV-E of the Social Security Act also requires every state to do criminal background checks of every prospective foster or adoptive parent, including specifically FBI checks. However, it does not mandate background checks for other adults living in the household. See Section 471(a)(20)(A) of the Social Security Act.

[64] Section 106(d) of CAPTA.

[65] As amended by P.L. 102-235 (1992), CAPTA provides that state grant funds are to be distributed "based on the population of children under the age of 18 in each State that

applies for a grant. . ." (see Section 106(a) of CAPTA). HHS has long interpreted this language to permit it to make a base allocation before distributing the remaining funds by population. Current distribution is described in HHS, ACF *Justifications of Estimates for the Appropriations Committees, FY2010*, p. 116.

[66] Certain tribal child protection issues are addressed in the Indian Child Protection and Family Violence Prevention Act of 1990 (P.L. 101-630).

[67] Planned national spending estimates, by purpose, were calculated by CRS based on state-by-state data included in "Compilation of State Child Welfare Expenditures Reported on CFS-101," submitted by HHS to Congress (August 2008).

[68] *Social Services Block Grant Program Annual Report 2007.* Available through the HHS, Administration for Children and Families, Office of Community Services at http://www.acf.hhs.gov/programs/ocs/ssbg/reports/2007/index.html.

[69] Ibid. For purposes of this reporting requirement, protective services for children is defined as "services or activities designed to prevent or remedy abuse, neglect, or exploitation of children who may be harmed through physical or mental injury, sexual abuse or exploitation, and negligent treatment or maltreatment, including failure to be provided with adequate food, clothing, shelter, or medical care. Component services or activities may include immediate investigation and intervention; emergency medical services; emergency shelter; developing case plans; initiation of legal action (if needed); counseling for the child and the family; assessment/evaluation of family circumstances; arranging alternative living arrangements; preparing for foster placement, if needed; and case management and referral to service providers."

[70] Ibid, Chapter 2. Use of SSBG funds for child protective services varies greatly by state.

[71] Section 201(b)(1)-(5) and Section 206(b) of CAPTA

[72] Section 206(a) of CAPTA.

[73] The statute also specifies the following services for which "access" is to be provided: child care, early childhood development and intervention services; self sufficiency and life management skills training; peer counseling; and community or direct referrals, including referrals for early developmental screening of children, services and supports to meet the additional needs of families with disabilities, adoption counseling for individuals seeking to adopt a child or to relinquish a child for adoption, job readiness services, and education services (e.g., tutoring, literacy, GED services).

[74] Section 202(1) of CAPTA.

[75] In two states (Oklahoma and Hawaii), however, the state public health department administers CBCAP funds.

[76] Lead agency information based on information available from CBCAP national resource center at http://www.friendsnrc.org/contacts/contacts.asp.

[77] Prior to the amendments made by the Keeping Children and Families Safe Act of 2003 (P.L. 108-36), assurance that the lead entity would provide these programs *through a network* was required, and that network was required to have interdisciplinary structures and balanced representation. Further, the lead entity was responsible for providing direction to this network. In explaining the deletion of "network" in multiple places, both the Senate HELP (S.Rept. 108-12, p. 17) and the House Education and Workforce (H.Rept. 108-26, p. 30) committees noted that "it is not the intent of the committee to alter State practices of funding networks or to de-emphasize the important role that networks can play in conducting prevention programs."

[78] Section 202(2)(A)-(C) and Section 202(3)(D) of CAPTA.

[79] Section 202(3)(A)-(C) of CAPTA.

[80] Section 205(1)-(3), (6)-(9) and (11) of CAPTA.

[81] Section 205(4) and (5) of CAPTA.

[82] Section 205(10) and (12) of CAPTA and Section 207 of CAPTA.

[83] Section 203(a) of CAPTA.

[84] Section 208 of CAPTA.

[85] The statute does not define "state" for purposes of these grants (Title II of CAPTA). In the absence of this definition, HHS uses the definition of state that applies to CAPTA state grants, which includes all 50 states, the District of Columbia, Puerto Rico, and four territories or "insular areas" (American Samoa, Guam, Northern Mariana Islands, and the U.S. Virgin Islands).

[86] Under the minimum allotment process, HHS distributes the available funds based on a state's relative share of the child population. In the event that this process results in any state receiving an allotment amount that is less than the minimum allotment amount, that state's actual population-based CBCAP funding is increased to the minimum amount by ratably reducing the amount of funds to any states with initial allotment above the minimum amount.

[87] The statute provides that no state may receive a CBCAP child population-based award of less than $175,000 (Section 203(b)(1)(A). However, beginning with FY2005, when the CBCAP appropriation increased by roughly $10 million, HHS has ensured that no state receives less than $200,000 in CBCAP child-population based funding.

[88] The insular areas (American Samoa, Guam, Northern Mariana Islands, and U.S. Virgin Islands) may each choose to receive CBCAP funds using a consolidated grant application. All currently do so and this both permits them to use CBCAP (and other program funds) for broad social service purposes (see 45 C.F.R. 97) and exempts them from the application requirements for CBCAP funds (e.g., appointment of lead entity to direct funding for community-based prevention activities). However, this makes them ineligible to claim any CBCAP leveraged funds awards.

[89] However, a state may choose to use the 20% matching funds it must provide on its CBCAP allotment as leverage funds provided, again, that those funds were not counted for matching or MOE purposes in any other federal program.

[90] The Children's Bureau sometimes pools CAPTA dollars with other research or technical assistance funding available for child welfare purposes and it funds a training and technical assistance network that covers a continuum of child welfare topics. For a complete listing see the "Training and Technical Assistance" section of the Children's Bureau webpage at http://www.acf.hhs.gov/programs/cb/tta/index.htm.

[91] The Children's Bureau jointly funds the National Center on Substance Abuse and Child Welfare with the Substance Abuse and Mental Health Services Administration (SAMHSA).

[92] Annual child maltreatment reports may be accessed from the Children's Bureau website at http://www.acf.hhs.gov/programs/cb/stats_research/index.htm#can. More information about the National Data Archive on Child Abuse and Neglect is available at http://www.acf.hhs.gov/programs/cb/tta/ndacan.htm.

[93] For information on discretionary grants see http://www.acf.hhs.gov/programs /cb/programs_fund/discretionary/captad.htm. For FY2006-FY2008 published priorities see *Federal Register* of February 3, 2006.

[94] The first National Incidence Survey was conducted in 1979-1980, a second was fielded in 1986-1987 and a third between 1993-1995. For more information see this website http://www.childwelfare.gov/systemwide/statistics/nis.cfm

[95] For more information see the NIS-4 website at https://www.nis4.org/nis4.asp.

[96] Section 101 of CAPTA.

[97] For more information on the working group and its membership see the information at the following website: http://www.acf.hhs.gov/programs/cb/fediawg/index.htm.

[98] Section 102 of CAPTA.

[99] The 1996 amendments to CAPTA (P.L. 104-235) removed this requirement from CAPTA and instead made appointment of an Advisory Board on Child Abuse and Neglect discretionary.

[100] A total of five reports were produced (1990, 1991, 1992, 1993, and 1995). See U.S. Department of Health and Human Services (HHS), *A Nation's Shame: Fatal Child Abuse and Neglect in the United States,* A Report of the U.S. Advisory Board on Child Abuse and Neglect (April 1995).

[101] See annual discretionary grants made by the Children's Bureau (beginning with FY2000) at this webpage http://www.acf.hhs.gov/programs/cb/programs_fund/discretionary/2008.htm. The awardees are shown for first full year of funding, although the duration of grants is typically 3 to 5 years. Grantees listed at this webpage include those who receive funding from the CAPTA discretionary account, as well as from other accounts administered by the Children's Bureau. However, grantees funded with CAPTA dollars are identified with the Catalog of Federal Domestic Assistance (CFDA) number 93.670.

[102] For FY2010 the Obama Administration requested continued funding for the initiative.

[103] For more information about the ACF home visitation initiative and other home visitation proposals in this Congress see CRS Report R40705, *Home Visitation for Families with Young Children*, by Emilie Stoltzfus and Karen E. Lynch.

[104] HHS, ASPE, *Interim Report to the Congress on the Feasibility of a National Child Abuse Registry*, May 2009. Available at http://aspe.hhs.gov/hsp/09/ChildAbuseRegistryInterimReport/index.shtml.

[105] There were no such earmarks identified in CAPTA's discretionary activities account in the FY2006 or FY2007 appropriations bills. However, for some earlier years, the earmarked funds were greater than those in the two most recent years. For example, out of the FY2004 appropriation $8.3 million was directed to support 25 projects in 13 states and for FY2005 $6.4 million was directed to support 21 projects in 12 states.

[106] The Crime Victims Funds was established by the Victims of Crime Act of 1984 (P.L. 98-473) and is administered by the Department of Justice. It consists primarily of fines collected from individuals convicted of federal crimes. The bulk of the funds distributed annually are provided to states for crime victim compensation and victim assistance programs. However, Section 1402(d)(2) of the Victims of Crime Act, as amended by the Child Abuse Prevention and Enforcement Act of 2000 (P.L. 106-177), provides that up to $20 million in funds must be set aside each year to support grants authorized under CAPTA to improve investigation, prosecution, and handling of child maltreatment cases.

[107] U.S. Department of Health and Human Services, Administration for Children and Families, "Availability of Fiscal Year 2009 Children's Justice Act Grants to States Under the Child Abuse Prevention and Treatment Act," Program Instructions, February 18, 2009 (ACYF-CB-PI-09-02), p. 7.

[108] Based on CRS communication with HHS, ACF.

[109] Each of the insular areas (American Samoa, Guam, Northern Mariana Islands, and U.S. Virgin Islands) are defined as states for purposes of this grant (Section 113 of CAPTA). However, under federal regulation (see 45 C.F.R. 97) they may each choose to receive Children's Justice Act funds using a consolidated grant application. All currently do so and this permits them to use these (and other) program funds for broad social service purposes and exempts them from specific application requirements for receipt of the Children's Justice Act funds (e.g., appointment of a multidisciplinary taskforce).

[110] Funds are distributed to tribes ($3 million) and to states and territories ($17 million). See more information at the Children's Bureau website http://www.acf.hhs.gov/programs/cb/programs_fund/state.

[111] These account names are from the official appropriations table that was included in the Explanatory Statement accompanying H.R. 1105 (which in this year has the effect of a conference agreement). See table at the end of *Division F*, (H.R. 1105, P.L. 111-8), p. 1720 at http://www.gpoaccess.gov/congress/house/appropriations/09conappro2.html.The exact names of the accounts may have varied slightly but the practice of appropriating CAPTA Title I dollars as two separate accounts is longstanding.

In: The Child Abuse Prevention and Treatment … ISBN: 978-1-62100-051-8
Editors: Craig S. Fiket, Amy W. Grotti

Chapter 2

DEFINITIONS OF CHILD ABUSE AND NEGLECT: SUMMARY OF STATE LAWS*

United States Department of Health and Human Services

Child abuse and neglect are defined by Federal and State laws. The Federal Child Abuse Prevention and Treatment Act (CAPTA) provides minimum standards that States must incorporate in their statutory definitions of child abuse and neglect. The CAPTA definition of "child abuse and neglect," at a minimum, refers to:

- "Any recent act or failure to act on the part of a parent or caretaker, which results in death, serious physical or emotional harm, sexual abuse, or exploitation, or an act or failure to act which presents an imminent risk of serious harm"[1]

The CAPTA definition of "sexual abuse" includes:

- "The employment, use, persuasion, inducement, enticement, or coercion of any child to engage in, or assist any other person to engage in, any sexually explicit conduct or simulation of such conduct for the purpose of producing a visual depiction of such conduct; or

---

* This website information has been edited, reformatted and augmented from www.childwelfare.gov/systemwide/laws_policies/statutes/defineall.cfm

- The rape, and in cases of caretaker or interfamilial relationships, statutory rape, molestation, prostitution, or other form of sexual exploitation of children, or incest with children"[2]

Types of Abuse

Nearly all States, the District of Columbia, American Samoa, Guam, the Northern Mariana Islands, Puerto Rico, and the U.S. Virgin Islands provide civil definitions of child abuse and neglect in statute.[3] As applied to reporting statutes, these definitions determine the grounds for intervention by State child protective agencies.[4] States recognize the different types of abuse in their definitions, including physical abuse, neglect, sexual abuse, and emotional abuse. Some States also provide definitions in statute for parental substance abuse and/or for abandonment as child abuse.

Physical Abuse

Physical abuse is generally defined as "any nonaccidental physical injury to the child" and can include striking, kicking, burning, or biting the child, or any action that results in a physical impairment of the child. In approximately 38 States and American Samoa, Guam, the Northern Mariana Islands, Puerto Rico, and the Virgin Islands, the definition of abuse also includes acts or circumstances that threaten the child with harm or create a substantial risk of harm to the child's health or welfare.[5]

Neglect

Neglect is frequently defined as the failure of a parent or other person with responsibility for the child to provide needed food, clothing, shelter, medical care, or supervision such that the child's health, safety, and well-being are threatened with harm. Approximately 24 States, the District of Columbia, American Samoa, Puerto Rico, and the Virgin Islands include failure to educate the child as required by law in their definition of neglect.[6] Seven States specifically define medical neglect as failing to provide any special medical treatment or mental health care needed by the child.[7] In addition, four

States define as medical neglect the withholding of medical treatment or nutrition from disabled infants with life-threatening conditions.[8]

Sexual Abuse/Exploitation

All States include sexual abuse in their definitions of child abuse. Some States refer in general terms to sexual abuse, while others specify various acts as sexual abuse. Sexual exploitation is an element of the definition of sexual abuse in most jurisdictions. Sexual exploitation includes allowing the child to engage in prostitution or in the production of child pornography.

Emotional Abuse

Almost all States, the District of Columbia, American Samoa, Guam, the Northern Mariana Islands, Puerto Rico, and the Virgin Islands include emotional maltreatment as part of their definitions of abuse or neglect.[9] Approximately 32 States, the District of Columbia, the Northern Mariana Islands, and Puerto Rico provide specific definitions of emotional abuse or mental injury to a child.[10] Typical language used in these definitions is "injury to the psychological capacity or emotional stability of the child as evidenced by an observable or substantial change in behavior, emotional response, or cognition," or as evidenced by "anxiety, depression, withdrawal, or aggressive behavior."

Parental Substance Abuse

Parental substance abuse is an element of the definition of child abuse or neglect in some States.[11] Circumstances that are considered abuse or neglect in some States include:

- Prenatal exposure of a child to harm due to the mother's use of an illegal drug or other substance (14 States and the District of Columbia)[12]
- Manufacture of a controlled substance in the presence of a child or on the premises occupied by a child (10 States)[13]

- Allowing a child to be present where the chemicals or equipment for the manufacture of controlled substances are used or stored (three States)[14]
- Selling, distributing, or giving drugs or alcohol to a child (seven States and Guam)[15]
- Use of a controlled substance by a caregiver that impairs the caregiver's ability to adequately care for the child (seven States)[16]

Abandonment

Approximately 17 States and the District of Columbia include abandonment in their definition of abuse or neglect, generally as a type of neglect.[17] Approximately 18 States, Guam, Puerto Rico, and the Virgin Islands provide definitions for abandonment that are separate from the definition of neglect.[18] In general, it is considered abandonment of the child when the parent's identity or whereabouts are unknown, the child has been left by the parent in circumstances in which the child suffers serious harm, or the parent has failed to maintain contact with the child or to provide reasonable support for a specified period of time.

Standards for Reporting

Generally speaking, a report must be made when an individual knows or has reasonable cause to believe or suspect that a child has been subjected to abuse or neglect. These standards guide mandatory reporters in deciding whether to make a report to child protective services.

Persons Responsible for the Child

In addition to defining acts or omissions that constitute child abuse or neglect, several States' statutes provide specific definitions of persons who can be reported to child protective services as perpetrators of abuse or neglect. These are persons who have some relationship or regular responsibility for the child. This generally includes parents, guardians, foster parents, relatives, or other caregivers responsible for the child's welfare.

EXCEPTIONS

A number of States provide exceptions in their reporting laws that exempt certain acts or omissions from their statutory definitions of child abuse and neglect. For instance, in 1 2 States and the District of Columbia, financial inability to provide for a child is exempted from the definition of neglect.[19] In 16 States, the District of Columbia, American Samoa, and the Northern Mariana Islands, physical discipline of a child, as long as it is reasonable and causes no bodily injury to the child, is an exception to the definition of abuse.[20]

The CAPTA amendments of 1996 added provisions specifying that nothing in the Act be construed as establishing a Federal requirement that a parent or legal guardian provide any medical service or treatment that is against the religious beliefs of the parent or legal guardian (42 U.S.C. § 51 06i). At the State level, 31 States, the District of Columbia, Guam, and Puerto Rico provide in their civil child abuse reporting laws an exception to the definition of child abuse and neglect for parents who choose not to seek medical care for their children due to religious beliefs.[21] However, 16 of the 31 States and Puerto Rico authorize the court to order medical treatment for the child when the child's condition warrants intervention.[22] Three States specifically provide an exception for Christian Science treatment.[23] Five States require mandated reporters to report instances when a child is not receiving medical care so that an investigation can be made.[24]

> This publication is a product of the State Statutes Series prepared by Child Welfare Information Gateway. While every attempt has been made to be as complete as possible, additional information on these topics may be in other sections of a State's code as well as agency regulations, case law, and informal practices and procedures.

Alabama

Physical Abuse

Citation: Ala. Code § 26-1 4-1 (1)-(3)

Abuse means harm or threatened harm to the health or welfare of a child through:

- Nonaccidental physical injury
- Sexual abuse or attempted sexual abuse
- Sexual exploitation or attempted sexual exploitation

Neglect

Citation: Ala. Code § 26-1 4-1 (1)-(3)

Neglect means negligent treatment or maltreatment of a child, including the failure to provide adequate food, clothing, shelter, medical treatment, or supervision.

Sexual Abuse/Exploitation

Citation: Ala. Code § 26-1 4-1 (1)-(3)

Sexual abuse includes:

- The employment, use, persuasion, inducement, enticement, or coercion of a child to engage in, or to have a child assist any other person to engage in sexually explicit conduct
- Any simulation of the conduct for the purpose of producing a visual depiction of the conduct
- The rape, molestation, prostitution, or other form of sexual exploitation of children
- Incest with children

Sexual exploitation includes:

- Allowing, permitting, or encouraging a child to engage in prostitution
- Allowing, permitting, encouraging, or engaging in obscene or pornographic photographing, filming, or depicting a child for commercial purposes

Emotional Abuse

Citation: Ala. Code § 26-1 4-1 (1)-(3)

The term *abuse* includes nonaccidental mental injury.

Abandonment

This issue is not addressed in the statutes reviewed.

Standards for Reporting

Citation: Ala. Code § 26-14-13

A report is required when the child is known or suspected to be a victim of child abuse or neglect.

Persons Responsible for the Child

Citation: Ala. Code § 26-1 4-7.2

Responsible persons include the child's parent or legal guardian.

Exceptions

Citation: Ala. Code § 26-1 4-7.2

A parent who fails to provide medical treatment to a child due to the legitimate practice of religious beliefs shall not be considered negligent for that reason alone. This exception shall not preclude a court from ordering that medical services be provided to the child.

Alaska

Physical Abuse

Citation: Alaska Stat. § 47.17.290

Child abuse or neglect means the physical injury or neglect, mental injury, sexual abuse, sexual exploitation, or maltreatment of a child under age 18 by a person under circumstances that indicate that the child's health or welfare is harmed or threatened.

Maltreatment means an act or omission that results in circumstances in which there is reasonable cause to suspect that a child may be a child in need of aid, as described in § 47.10.011, except that for purposes of this chapter, the act or omission need not have been committed by the child's parent, custodian, or guardian.

Neglect

Citation: Alaska Stat. § 47.17.290

Neglect means the failure of the person responsible for the child's welfare to provide the child necessary food, care, clothing, shelter, or medical attention.

Sexual Abuse/Exploitation

Citation: § 47.1 7.290

Child abuse or neglect includes sexual abuse or sexual exploitation.

Sexual exploitation includes the following conduct by a person responsible for the child's welfare:

- Allowing, permitting, or encouraging a child to engage in prostitution
- Allowing, permitting, or encouraging a child to engage in actual or simulated activities of a sexual nature that are prohibited by criminal statute

Emotional Abuse

Citation: Alaska Stat. § 47.17.290

Mental injury means a serious injury to the child as evidenced by an observable and substantial impairment in the child's ability to function in a developmentally appropriate manner and the existence of that impairment is supported by the opinion of a qualified expert witness.

Abandonment

This issue is not addressed in the statutes reviewed.

Standards for Reporting

Citation: Alaska Stat. § 47.17.020

A report is required when there is reasonable cause to suspect that a child has suffered harm as a result of child abuse or neglect.

Persons Responsible for the Child

Citation: Alaska Stat. § 47.17.290

A *person responsible for the child's welfare* includes:

- The child's parent, guardian, or foster parent
- The person responsible for the child's care at the time of the alleged child abuse or neglect
- The person responsible for the child's welfare in a public or private residential agency or institution

Exceptions

Citation: Alaska Stat. § 47.17.020(d)

A religious healing practitioner is not required to report as neglect of a child the failure to provide medical attention to the child if the child is provided treatment solely by spiritual means through prayer in accordance with the tenets and practices of a recognized church or religious denomination by an accredited practitioner of the church or denomination.

American Samoa

Physical Abuse

Citation: Ann. Code §§ 45.2001(a)(1); 46.3810

Abuse or *child abuse or neglect* means an act or omission that can include:

- Serious bruising, bleeding, malnutrition, failure to thrive, burns, fracture of a bone, subdural hematoma, soft tissue swelling, or death
- A condition or death that is not justifiably explained, or where the history given concerning the condition or death is at variance with the degree or type of condition or death, or circumstances indicate that the condition or death may not be the result of an accidental occurrence

Endangering the welfare of a child includes:

- Acts that create a substantial risk to the life, body, or health of a child less than 18 years old
- Any conduct that causes or tends to cause a substantial risk to the life, body, or health of the child
- Failure or refusal of the parent to exercise reasonable diligence in the care or control of the child to prevent a substantial risk to the life, body, or health of the child

Neglect

Citation: Ann. Code §§ 45.2001(a)(1); 45.0103

Abuse or *child abuse or neglect* means any case in which the child's parents, legal guardians, custodians, or any other person responsible for the child's health and welfare fail to take action to provide adequate food, clothing, shelter, medical care, or supervision that a prudent parent would take.

Neglected or dependent child means a child:

- Whose parent, guardian, or legal custodian has abandoned him or her or has subjected him or her to mistreatment or abuse or whose parent, guardian, or legal custodian has another to mistreat or abuse the child without taking lawful means to stop such mistreatment or abuse and to prevent it from recurring
- Who lacks proper parental care through the actions or omissions of the parent, guardian, or legal custodian
- Whose environment is injurious to his or her welfare
- Whose parent, guardian, or legal custodian fails or refuses to provide proper or necessary subsistence, education, medical care, or other care necessary for his or her health, guidance, or well-being
- Who is homeless, without proper care, or not domiciled with his or her parent, guardian, or legal custodian through no fault of his or her parent, guardian, or legal custodian

Sexual Abuse/Exploitation

Citation: Ann. Code § 45.2001 (a)(1)

The terms *abuse* or *child abuse or neglect* include an acts or omissions that can include when a child is:

- Subjected to sexual offenses, including rape, sexual assault, sexual abuse, or indecent exposure
- Allowed, permitted, or encouraged to engage in prostitution
- Allowed, permitted, or encouraged to be the subject of obscene or pornographic photographing, filming, or depicting

Emotional Abuse

Citation: Ann. Code § 45.2001 (a)(1)

The terms *abuse* or *child abuse or neglect* include mental injury.

Abandonment

This issue is not addressed in the statutes reviewed.

Standards for Reporting

Citation: Ann. Code § 45.2002

A report is required when there is reasonable cause to know or suspect that a child has been subjected to abuse or neglect.

Persons Responsible for the Child

Citation: Ann. Code §§ 45.2001(a)(1); 46.3805

Responsible persons include:

- The parent or guardian
- Any other person legally charged with the custody or care of a child
- Any person responsible for the child's health and welfare

Exceptions

Citation: Ann. Code § 45.2001 (a)(1)

Those investigating child abuse must take into account accepted child-rearing practices of the culture in which the child participates.

Reasonable exercise of parental discipline is not considered abuse. Normal parental discipline means all actions by parents, such as administration of blows by hand, strap, or light switch upon the buttocks, or any firm handling, scolding, or light taps, insufficient to seriously bruise or produce medical injury or disability.

Arizona

Physical Abuse

Citation: Rev. Stat. § 8-201

Abuse means:

- Inflicting or allowing physical injury, impairment of bodily function, or disfigurement
- Physical injury that results from permitting a child to enter or remain in any structure or vehicle in which volatile, toxic, or flammable chemicals are found or equipment is possessed by any person for the purpose of manufacturing a dangerous drug
- Unreasonable confinement of a child

Serious physical injury means an injury that is diagnosed by a medical doctor and that does any one or a combination of the following:

- Creates a reasonable risk of death
- Causes serious or permanent disfigurement
- Causes significant physical pain
- Causes serious impairment of health
- Causes the loss or protracted impairment of an organ or limb
- Is the result of sexual abuse, sexual conduct with a minor, sexual assault, molestation of a child, child prostitution, commercial sexual exploitation of a minor, sexual exploitation, or incest

Neglect

Citation: Rev. Stat. § 8-201

Neglect or *neglected* means:

- The inability or unwillingness of a parent, guardian, or custodian of a child to provide that child with supervision, food, clothing, shelter or medical care if that inability or unwillingness causes unreasonable risk of harm to the child's health or welfare
- Permitting a child to enter or remain in any structure or vehicle in which volatile, toxic, or flammable chemicals are found or equipment is possessed by any person for the purposes of manufacturing a dangerous drug
- A determination by a health professional that a newborn infant was exposed prenatally to a drug or substance listed in § 13-3401 and that this exposure was not the result of a medical treatment administered to the mother or the newborn infant by a health professional
- A diagnosis by a health professional of an infant under age 1 with clinical findings consistent with fetal alcohol syndrome or fetal alcohol effects

The determination by a health professional of prenatal exposure to a controlled substance shall be based on one or more of the following:

- Clinical indicators in the prenatal period, including maternal and newborn presentation
- History of substance use or abuse
- Medical history
- Results of a toxicology or other laboratory test on the mother or the newborn infant

Sexual Abuse/Exploitation

Citation: Rev. Stat. § 8-201

The term *abuse* includes:

- Inflicting or allowing sexual abuse
- Sexual conduct with a minor

- Sexual assault
- Molestation of a child
- Commercial sexual exploitation of a minor
- Sexual exploitation of a minor
- Incest
- Child prostitution

The term *neglect* includes:

- Deliberate exposure of a child by a parent, guardian, or custodian to sexual conduct, as defined in § 13-3551, or sexual contact, oral sexual contact, sexual intercourse, bestiality, or explicit sexual materials
- Any of the following acts committed by the child's parent, guardian, or custodian with reckless disregard as to whether the child is physically present:
    - Sexual contact
    - Oral sexual contact
    - Sexual intercourse
    - Bestiality

Emotional Abuse

Citation: Rev. Stat. § 8-201

The term *abuse* includes inflicting or allowing another person to cause serious emotional damage to a child, as evidenced by severe anxiety, depression, withdrawal, or untoward aggressive behavior, and such emotional damage is diagnosed by a medical doctor or psychologist, and the damage has been caused by the acts or omissions of an individual having care, custody, and control of a child.

Serious emotional injury means an injury that is diagnosed by a medical doctor or a psychologist and that does any one or a combination of the following:

- Seriously impairs mental faculties
- Causes serious anxiety, depression, withdrawal, or social dysfunction behavior to the extent that the child suffers dysfunction that requires treatment

- Is the result of sexual abuse, sexual conduct with a minor, sexual assault, molestation of a child, child prostitution, commercial sexual exploitation of a minor, sexual exploitation of a minor, or incest

Abandonment

Citation: Rev. Stat. § 8-201

Abandoned means:

- The failure of the parent to provide reasonable support and to maintain regular contact with the child, including providing normal supervision
- That a parent has made only minimal efforts to support and communicate with the child

Failure to maintain a normal parental relationship with the child without just cause for a period of 6 months shall constitute prima facie evidence of abandonment.

Standards for Reporting

Citation: Rev. Stat. § 13-3620

A report is required when a person reasonably believes that a child is or has been the victim of physical injury, abuse, or child abuse.

Persons Responsible for the Child

Citation: Rev. Stat. § 8-201

Responsible persons include:

- The parent
- A person having care, custody, and control of a child

Exceptions

Citation: Rev. Stat. § 8-201

A dependent child does not include a child who, in good faith, is being furnished Christian Science treatment by a duly accredited practitioner.

A child is not considered neglected if a parent's inability to meet the needs of the child is due solely to the unavailability of reasonable services.

Arkansas

Physical Abuse

Citation: Ann. Code § 12-18-103
Abuse means:

- Extreme or repeated cruelty to a child
- Engaging in conduct creating a realistic and serious threat of death, permanent or temporary disfigurement, or impairment of a bodily organ
- An injury that is at variance with the history given
- Any nonaccidental physical injury
- Any of the following acts with physical injury:
  - Throwing, kicking, burning, biting, or cutting a child
  - Striking a child with a closed fist
  - Shaking a child
  - Striking a child on the face or head
- Any of the following acts with or without physical injury:
  - Striking a child age 6 or younger on the face or head
  - Shaking a child age 3 or younger
  - Interfering with a child's breathing
  - Pinching, biting, or striking a child in the genital area
  - Tying a child to a fixed or heavy object or binding or tying a child's limbs together
  - Giving a child or permitting a child to consume or inhale a poisonous or noxious substance not prescribed by a physician that has the capacity to interfere with normal physiological functions
  - Giving a child or permitting a child to consume or inhale a substance not prescribed by a physician that has the capacity to alter the mood of the child, including, but not limited to, marijuana, alcohol for use other than during a recognized and established religious ceremony, a narcotic, or an over-the-counter

drug if a person purposely administers an overdose or an inappropriate drug and the child is detrimentally affected
- Exposing a child to dangerous chemicals including, but not limited to, a chemical used or generated during the manufacture of methamphetamine
- Subjecting a child to Munchausen syndrome by proxy or a factitious illness by proxy if the incident is confirmed by medical personnel

Neglect

Citation: Ann. Code § 12-18-103

Neglect means failure or refusal to:

- Prevent abuse of the child when the person knows or has reasonable cause to know the child is or has been abused
- Provide necessary food, clothing, shelter, and education required by law, or medical treatment necessary for the child's well-being
- Take reasonable action to protect the child from abandonment, abuse, sexual abuse, sexual exploitation, neglect, or parental unfitness when the existence of the condition was known or should have been known
- Provide for essential and necessary physical, mental, or emotional needs of the child, including the failure to provide a shelter that does not pose a risk to the health or safety of the child
- Provide for the child's care and maintenance, proper or necessary support, or medical, surgical, or other necessary care
- Assume responsibility for the care and custody of the child or to participate in a plan to assume such responsibility
- Appropriately supervise the child that results in the child being left alone at an inappropriate age or in inappropriate circumstances creating a dangerous situation or a situation that puts the child at risk of harm

Neglect shall also include:

- Causing a child to be born with an illegal substance in the child's bodily fluids or bodily substances as a result of the pregnant mother knowingly using an illegal substance before the birth of the child
- At the time of the birth of a child, the presence of an illegal substance in the mother's bodily fluids or bodily substances as a result of the

pregnant mother knowingly using an illegal substance before the birth of the child

- An *illegal substance* is a drug that is prohibited to be used or possessed without a prescription.
- A test of the child's or the mother's bodily fluids or bodily substances may be used as evidence to establish neglect.

Sexual Abuse/Exploitation

Citation: Ann. Code § 12-18-103

Sexual abuse means:

- By a person age 10 or older to a person younger than age 18:
    - Sexual intercourse, deviate sexual activity, or sexual contact by forcible compulsion
    - Attempted sexual intercourse, deviate sexual activity, or sexual contact by forcible compulsion
    - Indecent exposure
    - Forcing the watching of pornography or live sexual activity
- By a person age 18 or older to a person not his or her spouse who is younger than age 16:
    - Sexual intercourse, deviate sexual activity, or sexual contact
    - Attempted sexual intercourse, deviate sexual activity, or sexual contact
- By a caregiver to a person younger than age 18:
    - Sexual intercourse, deviate sexual activity, or sexual contact
    - Attempted sexual intercourse, deviate sexual activity, or sexual contact
    - Forcing or encouraging the watching of pornography
    - Forcing, permitting, or encouraging the watching of live sexual activity
    - Forcing the listening to a phone sex line
    - An act of voyeurism
- By a person younger than age 10 to a person younger than age 18:
    - Sexual intercourse, deviate sexual activity, or sexual contact by forcible compulsion
    - Attempted sexual intercourse, deviate sexual activity, or sexual contact by forcible compulsion

Sexual contact means an act of sexual gratification involving:

- Touching, directly or through clothing, the sex organs, buttocks, or anus of a person or the breast of a female
- Encouraging of a child to touch the offender in a sexual manner
- The offender requesting to touch a child in a sexual manner

Sexual exploitation means:

- Allowing, permitting, or encouraging participation or depiction of the child in prostitution, obscene photography, or obscene filming
- Obscenely depicting, posing, or posturing a child for any use or purpose

Emotional Abuse

Citation: Ann. Code § 12-18-103

The term *abuse* includes acts or omissions that result in injury to a child's intellectual, emotional, or psychological development, as evidenced by observable and substantial impairment of the child's ability to function within the child's normal range of performance and behavior.

Abandonment

Citation: Ann. Code § 12-18-103

Abandonment means:

- Failure of the parent to provide reasonable support and to maintain regular contact with the child through statement or contact, when the failure is accompanied by an intention on the part of the parent to permit the condition to continue for an indefinite period in the future
- Failure to support or maintain regular contact with the child without just cause
- An articulated intent to forgo parental responsibility

Standards for Reporting

Citation: Ann. Code § 12-18-402

A report is required when there is reasonable cause to suspect that a child has been subjected to child maltreatment.

Persons Responsible for the Child

Citation: Ann. Code § 12-18-103

Responsible persons include:

- A parent, guardian, or custodian
- A foster parent
- A person age 18 or older living in the child's home, whether related or unrelated
- A person who is entrusted with the child's care, including, but not limited to, an agent or employee of a public or private residential home, child care facility, public or private school, or any person legally responsible for the child's welfare

Exceptions

Citation: Ann. Code § 12-18-103

Abuse does not include physical discipline of a child when it is reasonable and moderate and is inflicted by a parent or guardian for purposes of restraining or correcting the child.

Abuse shall not include when a child suffers transient pain or minor temporary marks as the result of an appropriate restraint if:

- The person exercising the restraint is an employee of an agency licensed or exempted from licensure under the Child Welfare Agency Licensing Act.
- The agency has policy and procedures regarding restraints.
- No alternative exists to control the child except for a restraint.
- The child is in danger or hurting himself or herself or others.
- The person exercising the restraint has been trained properly in restraining children, de-escalation, and conflict resolution techniques.
- The restraint is for a reasonable period of time.

- The restraint is in conformity with training and agency policy and procedures.

Reasonable and moderate physical discipline inflicted by a parent or guardian shall not include an act that is likely to cause and that does cause injury more serious than transient pain or minor temporary marks.

The age, size, and condition of the child, the location of the injury, and the frequency or recurrence of injuries shall be considered when determining whether the physical discipline is reasonable or moderate.

It is not considered neglect when the parent's failure to provide for the child's needs is due to financial inability, and no services or relief have been offered.

California

Physical Abuse

Citation: Welf. & Inst. Code § 300

A child may be considered dependent when:

- The child has suffered, or there is a substantial risk that the child will suffer, serious physical harm inflicted nonaccidentally upon the child by the child's parent or guardian. For the purposes of this subdivision, a court may find there is a substantial risk of serious future injury based on the manner in which a less serious injury was inflicted, a history of repeated inflictions of injuries on the child or the child's siblings, or a combination of these and other actions by the parent or guardian that indicate the child is at risk of serious physical harm.
- The child is younger than age 5 and has suffered severe physical abuse by a parent or by any person known by the parent, if the parent knew or reasonably should have known that the person was physically abusing the child. For the purposes of this subdivision, *severe physical abuse* means:
  - Any single act of abuse that causes physical trauma of sufficient severity that, if left untreated, would cause permanent physical disfigurement, permanent physical disability, or death
  - Any single act of sexual abuse that causes significant bleeding, deep bruising, or significant external or internal swelling

    - More than one act of physical abuse, each of which causes bleeding, deep bruising, significant external or internal swelling, bone fracture, or unconsciousness
    - The willful, prolonged failure to provide adequate food
- The child's parent or guardian caused the death of another child through abuse or neglect.
- The child has been subjected to an act or acts of cruelty by the parent or guardian or a member of his or her household, or the parent or guardian has failed to adequately protect the child from an act or acts of cruelty when the parent or guardian knew or reasonably should have known that the child was in danger of being subjected to an act or acts of cruelty.

Neglect

Citation: Welf. & Inst. Code § 300

A child may be considered dependent when:

- The child has suffered, or there is a substantial risk that the child will suffer, serious physical harm or illness as a result of:
    - The failure or inability of the parent or guardian to adequately supervise or protect the child
    - The willful or negligent failure of the parent or guardian to adequately supervise or protect the child from the conduct of the custodian with whom the child has been left
    - The willful or negligent failure of the parent or guardian to provide the child with adequate food, clothing, shelter, or medical treatment
    - The inability of the parent or guardian to provide regular care for the child due to the parent's or guardian's mental illness, developmental disability, or substance abuse
- The child's sibling has been abused or neglected, and there is a substantial risk that the child will be abused or neglected. The court shall consider the circumstances surrounding the abuse or neglect of the sibling, the age and gender of each child, the nature of the abuse or neglect of the sibling, the mental condition of the parent or guardian, and any other factors the court considers probative in determining whether there is a substantial risk to the child.

Sexual Abuse/Exploitation

Citation: Welf. & Inst. Code § 300; Penal Code § 11165.1

A child is considered dependent if he or she has been sexually abused; there is a substantial risk that the child will be sexually abused, as defined in § 11165.1 of the Penal Code, by his or her parent, guardian, or a household member; or the parent or guardian has failed to adequately protect the child from sexual abuse when the parent or guardian knew or reasonably should have known that the child was in danger of sexual abuse.

Sexual abuse means sexual assault or sexual exploitation as defined below:

- *Sexual assault* includes rape, incest, sodomy, lewd or lascivious acts upon a child, or child molestation.
- *Sexual exploitation* refers to any of the following:
    - Depicting a minor engaged in obscene acts; preparing, selling, or distributing obscene matter that depicts minors; employing a minor to perform obscene acts
    - Knowingly permitting or encouraging a child to engage in, or assisting others to engage in, prostitution or a live performance involving obscene sexual conduct, or to either pose or model alone or with others for purposes of preparing a film, photograph, negative, slide, drawing, painting, or other pictorial depiction involving obscene sexual conduct
    - Depicting a child in, or knowingly developing, duplicating, printing, or exchanging any film, photograph, videotape, negative, or slide in which a child is engaged in an act of obscene sexual conduct

Emotional Abuse

Citation: Welf. & Inst. Code § 300

A child is considered dependent if he or she is suffering serious emotional damage, or is at substantial risk of suffering serious emotional damage, as evidenced by severe anxiety, depression, withdrawal, or untoward aggressive behavior toward self or others, as a result of the conduct of the parent or guardian, or who has no parent or guardian capable of providing appropriate care. No child shall be found to be a dependent person if the willful failure of the parent or guardian to provide adequate mental health treatment is based on a sincerely held religious belief and if a less intrusive judicial intervention is available.

Abandonment

Citation: Welf. & Inst. Code § 300

A child is considered dependent when:

- The child has been left without any provision for support.
- Physical custody of the child has been voluntarily surrendered pursuant to § 1255.7 of the Health and Safety Code, and the child has not been reclaimed within the 14-day period specified in subdivision (e) of that section.
- The child's parent has been incarcerated or institutionalized and cannot arrange for the care of the child.
- A relative or other adult custodian with whom the child resides or has been left is unwilling or unable to provide care or support for the child, the whereabouts of the parent are unknown, and reasonable efforts to locate the parent have been unsuccessful.
- The child has been freed for adoption by one or both parents for 12 months by either relinquishment or termination of parental rights or an adoption petition has not been granted.

Standards for Reporting

Citation: Penal Code § 11166

A report is required when there is a reasonable suspicion that a child is a victim of abuse or neglect.

Persons Responsible for the Child

Citation: Welf. & Inst. Code § 300

A person responsible for a child's welfare includes the child's parent or guardian. As used in this section, guardian means the legal guardian of the child.

Exceptions

Citation: Welf. & Inst. Code §§ 300; 300.5

Serious physical harm does not include reasonable and age-appropriate spanking to the buttocks where there is no evidence of serious physical injury.

No child shall be found to be dependent solely due to the lack of an emergency shelter for the family.

A physical disability, such as blindness or deafness, is not considered a bar to raising happy and well-adjusted children unless a parent's disability prevents him or her from exercising care and control.

A child whose parent has been adjudged a dependent child shall not be considered to be at risk of abuse or neglect solely because of the age, dependent status, or foster care status of the parent.

In any case in which a child is alleged to be dependent on the basis that he or she is in need of medical care, the court, in making that finding, shall give consideration to any treatment being provided to the child by spiritual means through prayer alone in accordance with the tenets and practices of a recognized church or religious denomination by an accredited practitioner thereof.

Colorado

Physical Abuse

Citation: Rev. Stat. § 19-1-103

Abuse or *child abuse or neglect* means an act or omission that threatens the health or welfare of a child in one of the following categories:

- Skin bruising, bleeding, malnutrition, failure to thrive, burns, fracture of any bone, subdural hematoma, soft tissue swelling, or death and either:
  - The condition or death is not justifiably explained.
  - The history given concerning the condition is at variance with the degree or type of such condition or death.
  - The circumstances indicate that the condition may not be the result of an accidental occurrence.
- A controlled substance is manufactured in the presence of a child, on the premises where a child is found, or where a child resides.

- A child tests positive at birth for either a schedule I or schedule II controlled substance, unless the child tests positive for a schedule II controlled substance as a result of the mother's lawful intake of such substance as prescribed.

Neglect

Citation: Rev. Stat. §§ 19-1-103; 19-3-102

The term *child abuse or neglect* includes any case in which a child is in need of services because the child's parent has failed to provide adequate food, clothing, shelter, medical care, or supervision that a prudent parent would take.

A child is *neglected* or *dependent* if:

- The parent, guardian, or legal custodian has subjected the child to mistreatment or abuse or has allowed another to mistreat or abuse the child without taking lawful means to stop such mistreatment or abuse and prevent it from recurring.
- The child lacks proper parental care through the actions or omissions of the parent, guardian, or legal custodian.
- The child's environment is injurious to his or her welfare.
- The parent, guardian, or legal custodian fails or refuses to provide the child with proper or necessary subsistence, education, medical care, or any other necessary care.
- The child is homeless, without proper care, or not domiciled with his or her parent, guardian, or legal custodian through no fault of such parent, guardian, or legal custodian.
- The child has run away from home or is otherwise beyond the control of his or her parent, guardian, or legal custodian.
- The child tests positive at birth for either a schedule I or schedule II controlled substance, unless the child tests positive for a schedule II controlled substance as a result of the mother's lawful intake of such substance as prescribed.

Sexual Abuse/Exploitation

Citation: Rev. Stat. § 19-1-103

Abuse or *child abuse or neglect* occurs when a child is subjected to sexual assault or molestation, sexual exploitation, or prostitution.

Sexual conduct includes any of the following:

- Sexual intercourse, including genital-genital, oral-genital, anal-genital, or oral-anal, whether between persons of the same or opposite sex or between humans and animals
- Penetration of the vagina or rectum by any object
- Masturbation
- Sexual sadomasochistic abuse

Emotional Abuse

Citation: Rev. Stat. § 19-1-103

The terms *abuse* or *child abuse or neglect* include any case in which a child is subjected to emotional abuse. Emotional abuse means an identifiable and substantial impairment or a substantial risk of impairment of the child's intellectual or psychological functioning or development.

Abandonment

Citation: Rev. Stat. § 19-3-102

A child is *neglected* or *dependent* if a parent, guardian, or legal custodian has abandoned the child.

Standards for Reporting

Citation: Rev. Stat. § 19-3-304

A report is required when there is reasonable cause to know or suspect that a child has been subjected to abuse or neglect.

Persons Responsible for the Child

Citation: Rev. Stat. § 19-1-103

Responsible person means a child's parent, legal guardian, custodian, or any other person responsible for the child's health and welfare.

Spousal equivalent means a person who is in a family-type living arrangement with a parent and who would be a stepparent if married to that parent.

Exceptions

Citation: Rev. Stat. §§ 19-1-103; 19-3-103

Those investigating cases of child abuse shall take into account child-rearing practices of the culture in which the child participates, including the work-related practices of agricultural communities.

The reasonable exercise of parental discipline is not considered abuse.

No child who, in lieu of medical treatment, is under treatment solely by spiritual means through prayer in accordance with a recognized method of religious healing shall, for that reason only, be considered neglected. The religious rights of the parent shall not limit the access of a child to medical care in a life-threatening situation.

Connecticut

Physical Abuse

Citation: Gen. Stat. § 46b-120

Effective January 1, 2010

The term *abused* means that a child or youth:

- Has been inflicted with physical injury or injuries by other than accidental means
- Has injuries that are at variance with the history given of them
- Is in a condition that is the result of maltreatment, that includes, but is not limited to, malnutrition, sexual molestation or exploitation, deprivation of necessities, emotional maltreatment, or cruel punishment

Neglect

Citation: Gen. Stat. § 46b-120

Effective January 1, 2010

A child or youth may be found *neglected* who:

- Has been abandoned
- Is being denied proper care and attention physically, educationally, emotionally, or morally

- Is being permitted to live under conditions, circumstances, or associations injurious to the well-being of the child or youth
- Has been abused

A child or youth may be found *uncared for* who is homeless or whose home cannot provide the specialized care that the physical, emotional, or mental condition of the child requires.

Sexual Abuse/Exploitation

Citation: Gen. Stat. § 46b-120

The term *abuse* includes sexual molestation or exploitation.

Emotional Abuse

Citation: Gen. Stat. § 46b-120

The term *abuse* includes emotional maltreatment.

Abandonment

Citation: Gen. Stat. § 46b-120

A child or youth may be found *neglected* who has been abandoned.

Standards for Reporting

Citation: Gen. Stat. § 17a-101a

A report is required when there is reasonable cause to suspect that a child has been abused or neglected.

Persons Responsible for the Child

Citation: Gen. Stat. § 46b-120

Responsible persons include the child's parents or guardian.

Exceptions

Citation: Gen. Stat. § 46b-120

The treatment of any child by an accredited Christian Science practitioner, in lieu of treatment by a licensed practitioner of the healing arts, shall not of itself constitute neglect or maltreatment.

Delaware

Physical Abuse

Citation: Ann. Code Tit. 16, § 902; Tit. 10, § 901

Abuse or *abused child* means a person:

- Causes or inflicts sexual abuse on a child
- Has care, custody, or control of a child, and causes or inflicts:
  - Physical injury through unjustified force
  - Emotional abuse
  - Torture
  - Exploitation
  - Maltreatment or mistreatment

Mistreatment or *maltreatment* are behaviors that inflict unnecessary or unjustifiable pain or suffering on a child without causing physical injury. Behaviors included consist of actions and omissions that are intentional and unintentional.

Neglect

Citation: Ann. Code Tit. 16, § 902; Tit. 10, § 901

Neglect or *neglected child* means that a person who is responsible for the care, custody, and/or control of the child and has the ability and financial means to provide for the care of the child:

- Fails to provide necessary food, clothing, shelter, education, health, medical, or other care necessary for the child's emotional, physical, or mental health, or safety and general well-being

- Chronically and severely abuses alcohol or a controlled substance, is not active in treatment for such abuse, and the abuse threatens the child's ability to receive care necessary for that child's safety and general well-being
- Fails to provide necessary and appropriate supervision for a child when the child is unable to care for his or her own basic needs or safety, after considering such factors as the child's age, mental ability, physical condition, the length of the caregiver's absence, and the context of the child's environment

Sexual Abuse/Exploitation

Citation: Ann. Code Tit. 16, § 902; Tit. 10, § 901

The term *abuse* includes sexual abuse and exploitation.

Sexual abuse means any act against a child that is described as a sex offense in § 761(g) of Title 11.

Exploitation means taking advantage of a child for unlawful or unjustifiable personal or sexual gain.

Emotional Abuse

Citation: Ann. Code Tit. 10, § 901

The term *abuse* includes emotional abuse. *Emotional abuse* means threats to inflict undue physical or emotional harm, and/or chronic or recurring incidents of ridiculing, demeaning, making derogatory remarks, or cursing.

Abandonment

This issue is not addressed in the statutes reviewed.

Standards for Reporting

Citation: Ann. Code Tit. 16, § 903

A report is required when a person knows or in good faith suspects child abuse or neglect.

Persons Responsible for the Child

Citation: Ann. Code Tit. 16, § 902; Tit. 10, § 901

Those responsible for care custody and control shall mean a person or persons in a position of trust, authority, supervision, or control over a child. They include:

- A parent, guardian, or custodian
- Other members of the child's family or household, including persons living together permanently or temporarily without regard to whether they are related to each other and without regard to the length of time or continuity of such residence, including persons who previously lived in the household such as paramours of a member of the child's household
- Any person who is defined as family or relatives, regardless of whether a member of the child's household
- Persons temporarily responsible for the child's well-being or care such as a health-care provider, aide, teacher, instructor, coach, sitter, day care or child care provider, or any other person having regular direct contact with children through affiliation with a school, church, or religious institution, health-care facility, athletic or charitable organization or any other organization whether such a person is compensated or acting as a volunteer
- Any person who has assumed control of or responsibility for the child

Exceptions

Citation: Ann. Code Tit. 16, § 913

No child who in good faith is under treatment solely by spiritual means through prayer in accordance with the practices of a recognized church or religious denomination shall for that reason alone be considered neglected.

District of Columbia

Physical Abuse

Citation: Ann. Code § 16-2301

Abused, when used in reference to a child, means:

- Infliction of physical or mental injury
- Sexual abuse or exploitation
- Negligent treatment or maltreatment

Neglect

Citation: Ann. Code § 16-2301

Neglected child means a child:

- Whose parent, guardian, or custodian has failed to make reasonable efforts to prevent the infliction of abuse upon the child
- Who is without proper parental care or control, subsistence, education, or other care or control necessary for his or her physical, mental, or emotional health
- Whose parent, guardian, or other custodian is unable to discharge his or her responsibilities to and for the child because of incarceration, hospitalization, or other physical or mental incapacity
- Whose parent, guardian, or custodian refuses or is unable to assume responsibility for the child's care, control, or subsistence and the person or institution providing for the child states an intention to discontinue such care
- Who is in imminent danger of being abused and another child living in the same household has been abused
- Who has received negligent treatment or maltreatment
- Who has resided in a hospital located in the District of Columbia for at least 10 calendar days following the its birth, despite a medical determination that the child is ready for discharge from the hospital, and the parent has not taken any action or made any effort to maintain a parental, guardianship, or custodial relationship or contact with the child

- Who is born addicted or dependent on a controlled substance or has a significant presence of a controlled substance in his or her system at birth
- In whose body there is a controlled substance as a direct and foreseeable consequence of the acts or omissions of the child's parent
- Who is regularly exposed to illegal drug-related activity in the home

Negligent treatment or *maltreatment* means failure to provide adequate food, clothing, shelter, or medical care that includes medical neglect, and the deprivation is not due to the lack of financial means of his or her parent, guardian, or other custodian.

Sexual Abuse/Exploitation

Citation: Ann. Code § 16-2301

Sexual abuse means:

- Engaging in, or attempting to engage in, a sexual act or sexual contact with a child
- Causing or attempting to cause a child to engage in sexually explicit conduct
- Exposing the child to sexually explicit conduct

Sexual exploitation occurs when a parent, guardian, or other custodian allows a child to engage in prostitution, or engages a child or allows a child to engage in obscene or pornographic photography, filming, or other forms of illustrating or promoting sexual conduct.

Emotional Abuse

Citation: Ann. Code § 16-2301

Mental injury means harm to a child's psychological or intellectual functioning that may be exhibited by severe anxiety, depression, withdrawal, outwardly aggressive behavior, or a combination of those behaviors, and that may be demonstrated by a change in behavior, emotional response, or cognition.

Abandonment

Citation: Ann. Code § 16-2301

The term *neglected child* includes a child who has been abandoned by his or her parent, guardian, or custodian.

Standards for Reporting

Citation: Ann. Code § 4-1321.02

A report is required when a person knows or has reasonable cause to suspect that a child has been or is in immediate danger of being a mentally or physically abused or neglected child.

Persons Responsible for the Child

Citation: Ann. Code § 16-2301

Responsible persons include a parent, guardian, or custodian.

Exceptions

Citation: Ann. Code § 16-2301

It is not neglect when the child's deprivation of parental care and control is due to a lack of financial means.

No child who in good faith is under treatment solely by spiritual means through prayer, in accordance with the practices of a recognized church or religious denomination by a duly accredited practitioner, shall for that reason alone be considered neglected.

The term *abused* does not include parental discipline, as long as the discipline is reasonable in manner and moderate in degree, and otherwise does not constitute cruelty. The term *discipline* does not include:

- Burning, biting, or cutting a child
- Striking a child with a closed fist
- Inflicting injury to a child by shaking, kicking, or throwing the child
- Nonaccidental injury to a child younger than 18 months
- Interfering with a child's breathing
- Threatening a child with a dangerous weapon or using such a weapon on a child

Florida

Physical Abuse

Citation: Ann. Stat. § 39.01

Abuse means any willful act or threatened act that results in any physical, mental, or sexual injury or harm that causes or is likely to cause a child's physical, mental, or emotional health to be significantly impaired. Abuse of a child includes acts or omissions.

Harm to a child's health or welfare can occur when a person:

- Inflicts or allows to be inflicted upon the child physical, mental, or emotional injury
- Purposely gives a child poison, alcohol, drugs, or other substances that substantially affect the child's behavior, motor coordination, or judgment or that result in sickness or internal injury
- Leaves a child without adult supervision or arrangement appropriate for the child's age or mental or physical condition
- Uses inappropriate or excessively harsh discipline that is likely to result in physical injury, mental injury as defined in this section, or emotional injury
- Commits or allows to be committed sexual battery against the child
- Allows, encourages, or forces the sexual exploitation of a child
- Abandons the child
- Neglects the child
- Exposes a child to a controlled substance or alcohol
- Uses mechanical devices, unreasonable restraints, or extended periods of isolation to control a child
- Engages in violent behavior that demonstrates a wanton disregard for the presence of a child and could reasonably result in serious injury to the child
- Negligently fails to protect a child in his or her care from inflicted physical, mental, or sexual injury caused by the acts of another
- Has allowed a child's sibling to die as a result of abuse, abandonment, or neglect
- Makes the child unavailable for the purpose of impeding or avoiding a protective investigation unless the court determines that the parent,

legal custodian, or caregiver was fleeing from a situation involving domestic violence

Neglect

Citation: Ann. Stat. § 39.01

Neglect occurs when a child is deprived of, or is allowed to be deprived of, necessary food, clothing, shelter, or medical treatment or a child is permitted to live in an environment when such deprivation or environment causes the child's physical, mental, or emotional health to be significantly impaired or to be in danger of being significantly impaired.

Sexual Abuse/Exploitation

Citation: Ann. Stat. § 39.01

Sexual abuse of a child means one or more of the following acts:

- Any penetration, however slight, of the vagina or anal opening of one person by the penis of another person, whether or not there is the emission of semen
- Any sexual contact between the genitals or anal opening of one person and the mouth or tongue of another person
- Any intrusion by one person into the genitals or anal opening of another person, including the use of any object for this purpose, not including any act intended for a valid medical purpose
- The intentional touching of the genitals or intimate parts, including the breasts, genital area, groin, inner thighs, and buttocks, or the clothing covering them, of either the child or the perpetrator, not including:
    - An act that may reasonably be construed to be a normal caregiver responsibility or any interaction with or affection for a child
    - An act intended for a valid medical purpose
- The intentional masturbation of the perpetrator's genitals in the presence of a child
- The intentional exposure of the perpetrator's genitals in the presence of a child, or any other sexual act intentionally perpetrated in the presence of a child, if such exposure or sexual act is for the purpose of

sexual arousal or gratification, aggression, degradation, or other similar purpose

- The sexual exploitation of a child, including allowing, encouraging, or forcing a child to solicit for or engage in prostitution or engage in a sexual performance

Emotional Abuse

Citation: Ann. Stat. § 39.01

Mental injury means an injury to the intellectual or psychological capacity of a child as evidenced by a discernible and substantial impairment in the ability to function within the normal range of performance and behavior.

Abandonment

Citation: Ann. Stat. § 39.01

Abandoned or *abandonment* occurs when the parent or legal custodian of a child or, in the absence of a parent or legal custodian, the caregiver, while being able, makes no provision for the child's support and has failed to establish or maintain a substantial and positive relationship with the child.

For purposes of this subsection, *establish* or *maintain a substantial and positive relationship* includes, but is not limited to, frequent and regular contact with the child through frequent and regular visitation or frequent and regular communication to or with the child, and the exercise of parental rights and responsibilities. Marginal efforts and incidental or token visits or communications are not sufficient to establish or maintain a substantial and positive relationship with a child.

The term does not include a surrendered newborn infant as described in § 383.50, a *child in need of services* or a *family in need of services* as defined in chapter 984. The incarceration of a parent, legal custodian, or caregiver responsible for a child's welfare may support a finding of abandonment.

Standards for Reporting

Citation: Ann. Stat. § 39.201

A report is required when a person knows, or has reasonable cause to suspect, that a child is abused, abandoned, or neglected.

Persons Responsible for the Child

Citation: Ann. Stat. § 39.01

Responsible persons include the child's parent or legal custodian, or, in the absence of the parent or legal custodian, the child's caregiver. The term *caregiver* includes the parent, legal custodian, adult household member, or other person responsible for a child's welfare.

Other person responsible for a child's welfare includes:

- The child's legal guardian or foster parent
- An employee of a private school, public or private child daycare center, residential home, institution, facility, or agency
- A law enforcement officer employed in any facility, service, or program for children that is operated or contracted by the Department of Juvenile Justice
- Any other person legally responsible for the child's welfare in a residential setting
- An adult sitter or relative entrusted with a child's care

Exceptions

Citation: Ann. Stat. § 39.01

Corporal discipline of a child by a parent does not in itself constitute abuse when it does not result in harm to the child.

It shall not be considered neglect if failure to provide for the child is caused primarily by financial inability unless actual services for relief have been offered to and rejected by the parent.

A parent legitimately practicing religious beliefs in accordance with a recognized church or religious organization who does not provide specific medical treatment for a child may not, for that reason alone, be considered a negligent parent. This exception does not preclude a court from ordering medical services or other treatment to be provided when the health of the child so requires.

Georgia

Physical Abuse

Citation: Ann. Code § 19-7-5(b)

Child abuse means physical injury or death inflicted upon a child by a parent or caregiver by other than accidental means.

Neglect

Citation: Ann. Code § 19-7-5(b)

The term *child abuse* includes neglect or exploitation of a child by a parent or caregiver.

Sexual Abuse/Exploitation

Citation: Ann. Code § 19-7-5(b)

Sexual abuse occurs when a person employs, uses, persuades, induces, entices, or coercesg a minor who is not that person's spouse to engage in any act that involves:

- Sexual intercourse, including genital-genital, oral-genital, anal-genital, or oral-anal, whether between persons of the same or opposite sex
- Bestiality or masturbation
- Lewd exhibition of the genitals or pubic area of any person
- Flagellation or torture by or upon a person who is nude
- Condition of being fettered, bound, or otherwise physically restrained on the part of a person who is nude
- Physical contact in an act of apparent sexual stimulation or gratification with any person's clothed or unclothed genitals, pubic area, or buttocks or with a female's clothed or unclothed breasts
- Defecation or urination for the purpose of sexual stimulation
- Penetration of the vagina or rectum by any object except when done as part of a recognized medical procedure

Sexual exploitation means conduct by any person who allows, permits, encourages, or requires a child to engage in prostitution or sexually explicit conduct for the purpose of producing a visual or print medium depicting such conduct.

Emotional Abuse

This issue is not addressed in the statutes reviewed.

Abandonment

This issue is not addressed in the statutes reviewed.

Standards for Reporting

Citation: Ann. Code § 19-7-5(b)

A report is required when there is reasonable cause to believe that a child is abused.

Persons Responsible for the Child

Citation: Ann. Code § 19-7-5(b)

The term *responsible person* includes the parent or caregiver.

Exceptions

Citation: Ann. Code § 19-7-5(b)

Physical forms of discipline may be used as long as there is no physical injury to the child.

No child who in good faith is being treated solely by spiritual means through prayer in accordance with the tenets and practices of a recognized church or religious denomination by a duly accredited practitioner thereof shall, for that reason alone, be considered to be an abused child.

Sexual abuse does not include consensual sex acts between persons of the opposite sex who are minors or a minor and adult who is no more than 5 years older than the minor.

Guam

Physical Abuse

Citation: Ann. Code Tit. 19, § 13101

Abused or neglected child means a child whose physical or mental health or welfare is harmed or threatened with harm by the acts or omissions of the person or persons responsible for the child's welfare.

Harm to a child's physical health or welfare occurs in cases in which there exists evidence of injury, including but not limited to:

- A case in which the child exhibits evidence of skin bruising or other internal bleeding, an injury to skin causing bleeding, burns, poisoning, fracture of any bone, subdural hematoma, soft tissue swelling, extreme pain, or death
- Disfigurement or impairment of a bodily organ, and such injury is inflicted by other than accidental means, by excessive corporal punishment, or where the history given concerning such condition or death is at variance with the degree or type of such condition or death
- A case in which the child is provided with a controlled substance, except for drugs prescribed by a medical practitioner

Neglect

Citation: Ann. Code Tit. 19, § 13101

The term *abused or neglected child* includes a child whose physical or mental health or welfare is harmed or threatened with harm by the acts or omissions of the person or persons responsible for the child's welfare.

Harm to a child's physical health or welfare includes a case in which the physical health of the child is adversely affected because the person responsible for the child's welfare has not regularly provided the child, in a timely manner, with adequate food, clothing, shelter, psychological care, physical care, health care, or supervision, when able to financially or if offered financial assistance, health care, or other reasonable means to do so.

Sexual Abuse/Exploitation

Citation: Ann. Code Tit. 19, § 13101

Harm to a child's physical health or welfare occurs in a case in which there exists evidence of injury, including but not limited to a case in which the child has been the victim of a sexual offense, as defined in the Criminal and Correctional Code.

Emotional Abuse

Citation: Ann. Code Tit. 19, § 13101

The term *abused or neglected child* includes a child whose mental health or welfare is harmed or threatened with harm by the acts or omissions of the person or persons responsible for the child's welfare.

Harm occurs when there exists injury to the psychological capacity of a child such as failure to thrive, extreme mental distress, or gross emotional or verbal degradation, as is evidenced by an observable and substantial impairment in the child's ability to function within a normal range of performance with due regard to the child's culture.

Abandonment

Citation: Ann. Code Tit. 19, § 13101

Abandonment means the desertion or willful forsaking of a minor by the person responsible for the child's welfare under circumstances in which a reasonable person would continue to provide care or custody.

The term *harm* includes a case in which the child has been abandoned.

Standards for Reporting

Citation: Ann. Code Tit. 19, § 13202

A report must be made when there is reasonable cause to suspect that a child is an abused or neglected child.

Persons Responsible for the Child

Citation: Ann. Code Tit. 19, § 13101

A *person responsible for the child's welfare* includes:

- The child's parent, guardian, or foster parent
- An employee of a public or private residential home or an institution or authorized agency responsible for the child's welfare

The term *family* includes each legal parent, the grandparents, each parent's spouse, each sibling or person related by consanguinity up to the second degree or by marriage, each person residing in the same dwelling unit, and any other person or legal entity that is a child's legal or physical custodian or guardian, or who is otherwise responsible for the child's care.

Exceptions

Citation: Ann. Code Tit. 19, § 13101

A person responsible for the child's welfare who, while legitimately practicing his or her religious beliefs, does not specify medical treatment for the child should not for that reason alone be considered as harming or threatening harm to the child.

Hawaii

Physical Abuse

Citation: Rev. Stat. § 350-1

Child abuse or neglect means acts or omissions that have resulted in the physical health or welfare of the child, who is under age 18, to be harmed or to be subject to a reasonably foreseeable, substantial risk of being harmed. The acts or omissions are indicated for the purposes of reports by circumstances that include but are not limited to:

- When the child exhibits evidence of any of the following injuries, and such injury is not justifiably explained, or when the history given concerning such condition or death is at variance with the degree or

type of such condition or death, or circumstances indicate that such condition or death may not be the product of an accidental occurrence:
    - Substantial or multiple skin bruising or other internal bleeding
    - An injury to skin causing substantial bleeding
    - Malnutrition or failure to thrive
    - Burns or poisoning
    - Fracture of any bone
    - Subdural hematoma or soft tissue swelling
    - Extreme pain or mental distress
    - Gross degradation
    - Death
- When the child is provided with dangerous, harmful, or detrimental drugs; provided that this paragraph shall not apply when such drugs are provided to the child pursuant to the direction or prescription of a practitioner

Neglect

Citation: Rev. Stat. § 350-1

Child neglect occurs when a child is not provided in a timely manner with adequate food, clothing, shelter, psychological care, physical care, medical care, or supervision.

Sexual Abuse/Exploitation

Citation: Rev. Stat. § 350-1

The term *child abuse or neglect* includes instances when the child has been the victim of:

- Sexual contact or conduct including, but not limited to, sexual assault
- Molestation or sexual fondling
- Incest
- Prostitution
- Obscene or pornographic photographing, filming, or depiction, or other similar forms of sexual exploitation

Emotional Abuse

Citation: Rev. Stat. § 350-1

The term *child abuse or neglect* includes acts or omissions that have resulted in injury to the psychological capacity of a child as is evidenced by an observable and substantial impairment in the child's ability to function.

Abandonment

This issue is not addressed in the statutes reviewed.

Standards for Reporting

Citation: Rev. Stat. § 350-1.1

A report is required when there is reason to believe that child abuse or neglect has occurred or that there exists a substantial risk that child abuse or neglect may occur in the reasonably foreseeable future.

Persons Responsible for the Child

Citation: Rev. Stat. § 350-1

A *responsible person* is any person who, or legal entity that, is:

- In any manner or degree related to the child
- Residing with the child
- Otherwise responsible for the child's care

Exceptions

No exceptions are specified in statute.

Idaho

Physical Abuse

Citation: Idaho Code § 16-1602

Abused means any case in which a child has been the victim of conduct or omission resulting in skin bruising, bleeding, malnutrition, burns, fracture of any bone, subdural hematoma, soft tissue swelling, failure to thrive, or death, and such condition or death is not justifiably explained; the history given concerning such condition or death is at variance with the degree or type of such condition or death; or the circumstances indicate that such condition or death may not be the product of an accidental occurrence.

Neglect

Citation: Idaho Code § 16-1602

Neglected means a child:

- Who is without proper parental care and control, subsistence, medical, or other care necessary for his or her wellbeing because of the conduct or omission of his or her parents, guardian, or other custodian, or their neglect or refusal to provide them
- Whose parents, guardian, or other custodian is unable to discharge his or her responsibilities to and for the child and, as a result of such inability, the child lacks the parental care necessary for his or her health, safety, or well-being
- Who has been placed for care or adoption in violation of the law
- Who is without proper education because of the failure to comply with § 33-202

Sexual Abuse/Exploitation

Citation: Idaho Code § 16-1602

The term *abused* applies to any case in which a child has been the victim of sexual conduct, including rape, molestation, incest, prostitution, obscene or pornographic photographing, filming or depiction for commercial purposes, or other similar forms of sexual exploitation that harms or threatens the child's health, welfare, or mental health.

Emotional Abuse

Citation: Idaho Code § 16-1602

Mental injury means a substantial impairment in the intellectual or psychological ability of a child to function within a normal range of performance and/or behavior, for short or long terms.

Abandonment

Citation: Idaho Code § 16-1602

Abandoned means the failure of the parent to maintain a normal parental relationship with his or her child, including but not limited to reasonable support or regular personal contact. Failure to maintain this relationship without just cause for a period of 1 year shall constitute *prima facie* evidence of abandonment.

Standards for Reporting

Citation: Idaho Code § 16-1605

A report is required when there is reason to believe that a child younger than age 18 has been abused, abandoned, or neglected.

Persons Responsible for the Child

Citation: Idaho Code § 16-1602

Responsible persons include the parent, guardian, or other custodian.

Exceptions

Citation: Idaho Code § 16-1602

No child whose parent chooses for the child treatment by prayers through spiritual means alone in lieu of medical treatment shall be deemed for that reason alone to be neglected. This exception shall not prevent the court from ordering emergency medical treatment when the child's life is endangered.

Illinois

Physical Abuse

Citation: Comp. Stat. Ch. 325, § 5/3

Abused child means a child whose parent, immediate family member, any person responsible for the child's welfare, any individual residing in the same home as the child, or a paramour of the child's parent:

- Inflicts, causes or allows to be inflicted, or creates a substantial risk of physical injury by other than accidental means, that causes death, disfigurement, impairment of physical or emotional health, or loss or impairment of any bodily function
- Commits or allows to be committed an act or acts of torture upon the child
- Inflicts excessive corporal punishment
- Commits or allows to be committed the offense of female genital mutilation
- Causes a controlled substance to be sold, transferred, distributed, or given to the child under age 18, in violation of the Illinois Controlled Substances Act or Methamphetamine Control and Community Protection Act

Neglect

Citation: Comp. Stat. Ch. 325, § 5/3

Neglected child means any child who:

- Is not receiving proper or necessary nourishment or medically indicated treatment, including food or care, that is not provided solely on the basis of the present or anticipated mental or physical impairment as determined by a physician, or otherwise is not receiving the proper or necessary support or medical or other remedial care as necessary for a child's well-being
- Is not receiving other care necessary for his or her well-being, including adequate food, clothing, and shelter
- Has been provided with interim crisis intervention services under chapter 705, § 405/3-5 and whose parent, guardian, or custodian refuses to permit the child to return home and no other living arrangement agreeable to the parent, guardian, or custodian can be made, and the parent, guardian, or custodian has not made any other appropriate living arrangement for the child
- Is a newborn infant whose blood, urine, or meconium contains any amount of a controlled substance or a metabolite thereof

Sexual Abuse/Exploitation

Citation: Comp. Stat. Ch. 325, § 5/3

The term *abused child* includes a child whose parent, immediate family member, person responsible for the child's welfare, individual residing in the same home as the child, or paramour of the child's parent commits or allows to be committed any sex offense against the child.

Emotional Abuse

Citation: Comp. Stat. Ch. 325, § 5/3

The term *abused child* includes impairment or substantial risk of impairment to the child's emotional health.

Abandonment

Citation: Comp. Stat. Ch. 325, § 5/3

The term *neglected child* includes a child who is abandoned by his or her parents or other person responsible for the child's welfare without a proper plan of care.

Standards for Reporting

Citation: Comp. Stat. Ch. 325, § 5/4

A report is required when there is reasonable cause to believe that a child may be an abused or neglected child.

Persons Responsible for the Child

Citation: Comp. Stat. Ch. 325, § 5/3

A *person responsible for the child's welfare* includes:

- The child's parent, guardian, foster parent, or relative caregiver
- Any person responsible for the child's welfare in a public or private residential agency, institution, or child care facility
- Any other person responsible for the child's welfare at the time of the alleged abuse or neglect, including an immediate family member, any

person residing in the child's home, or a paramour of the child's parent
- A person who came to know the child through an official capacity or position of trust, including but not limited to health-care professionals, educational personnel, recreational supervisors, members of the clergy, and volunteers or support personnel in any setting where children may be subject to abuse or neglect

Exceptions

Citation: Comp. Stat. Ch. 325, § 5/3

A child shall not be considered abused or neglected if:

- The child is a newborn who has been relinquished in accordance with the Abandoned Newborn Infant Protection Act.
- The presence of a controlled substance in a child or a newborn is the result of medical treatment.
- The child has been left in the care of an adult relative.
- The child's parent relies on spiritual means through prayer for the treatment of disease.
- The child is not attending school as required by the School Act.

Indiana

Physical Abuse

Citation: Ann. Code § 31-34-1-2

A child is a *child in need of services* if, before the child becomes age 18, the child's physical or mental health is seriously endangered due to injury by the act or omission of the child's parent, guardian, or custodian.

Evidence that the illegal manufacture of a drug or controlled substance is occurring on property where a child resides creates a rebuttable presumption that the child's physical or mental health is seriously endangered.

Neglect

Citation: Ann. Code §§ 31-34-1-1; 31-34-1-9; 31-34-1-10; 31-34-1-11

A child is a *child in need of services* if, before the child becomes age 18:

- The child's physical or mental condition is seriously impaired or seriously endangered as a result of the inability, refusal, or neglect of the child's parent, guardian, or custodian to supply the child with necessary food, clothing, shelter, medical care, education, or supervision.
- The child is born with fetal alcohol syndrome, or any amount, including a trace amount, of a controlled substance or a legend drug in the child's body.
- The child has an injury, abnormal physical or psychological development, or is at a substantial risk of a life- threatening condition that arises or is substantially aggravated because the child's mother used alcohol, a controlled substance, or a legend drug during pregnancy.

A *child in need of services* includes a child with a disability who is deprived of nutrition that is necessary to sustain life, or is deprived of medical or surgical intervention that is necessary to remedy or ameliorate a life-threatening medical condition if the nutritional, medical, or surgical intervention is generally provided to similarly situated children with or without disabilities.

Sexual Abuse/Exploitation

Citation: Ann. Code §§ 31-34-1-3; 31-34-1-4; 31-34-1-5

A child is a *child in need of services* if, before the child becomes age 18, the child is the victim, lives in the same household as another child who was the victim, or lives in the same household as the adult who was convicted of a sex offense, as defined in the criminal statutes, pertaining to:

- Rape
- Criminal deviate conduct
- Child molesting
- Child exploitation or possession of child pornography

- Child seduction
- Sexual misconduct with a minor
- Indecent exposure
- Prostitution
- Incest

A child is a child in need of services if, before the child becomes age 18, the child's parent, guardian, or custodian allows the child:

- To participate in an obscene performance
- To commit a sex offense prohibited by criminal statute

Emotional Abuse

Citation: Ann. Code § 31-34-1-2

A child is a *child in need of services* if the child's mental health is seriously endangered by the act or omission of the child's parent, guardian, or custodian.

Abandonment

Citation: Ann. Code § 31-9-2-0.5

Abandoned infant means:

- A child who is less than 12 months old and whose parent, guardian, or custodian has knowingly or intentionally left the child in an environment that endangers the child's life or heath or in a hospital or medical facility and has no reasonable plan to assume the care, custody, and control of the child
- A child who is, or appears to be, not more than 45 days old and whose parent has knowingly and intentionally left the child with an emergency medical services provider and did not express an intent to return for the child

Standards for Reporting

Citation: Ann. Code § 31-33-51

A report is required when an individual has reason to believe that a child is a victim of child abuse or neglect.

Persons Responsible for the Child

Citation: Ann. Code §§ 31-9-2-0.5; 31-34-1-1 through 31-34-1-5

Responsible persons include the child's parent, guardian, or custodian.

Exceptions

Citation: Ann. Code §§ 31-34-1-12; 31-34-1-14; 31-34-1-15

A child is not a child in need of services if:

- The presence of a controlled substance was from a valid medical prescription.
- A parent fails to provide specific medical treatment for a child because of legitimate and genuine religious beliefs. This presumption does not do any of the following:
    - Prevent a court from ordering medical services when the health of the child requires it
    - Apply to situations in which the child's life or health is in serious danger

This chapter does not limit:

- The right of the parent to use reasonable corporal punishment to discipline the child
- The lawful practice or teaching of religious beliefs

Iowa

Physical Abuse

Citation: Ann. Stat. § 232.68

Child abuse or *abuse* means any nonaccidental physical injury, or injury that is at variance with the history given of it, suffered by a child as the result of acts or omissions of a person responsible for the care of the child.

Neglect

Citation: Ann. Stat. § 232.68

The terms *child abuse* or *abuse* include:

- The failure on the part of a person responsible for the care of a child to provide adequate food, shelter, clothing, or other care necessary for the child's health and welfare when financially able to do so or when offered financial or other reasonable means to do so
- The presence of an illegal drug in a child's body as a direct and foreseeable consequence of the acts or omissions of the person responsible for the care of the child
- That the person responsible for the care of a child has, in the presence of the child, manufactured a dangerous substance or possesses a product containing ephedrine, its salts, optical isomers, salts of optical isomers, or pseudoephedrine, its salts, optical isomers, or salts of optical isomers, with the intent to use the product as a precursor or an intermediary to a dangerous substance
- Knowingly allowing a person to have custody or control of, or unsupervised access to a child after knowing the person is required to register or is on the sex offender registry

Sexual Abuse/Exploitation

Citation: Ann. Stat. § 232.68

The terms *child abuse* or *abuse* include:

- Committing of a sexual offense with or to a child
- Allowing, permitting, or encouraging the child to engage in prostitution
- Committing of bestiality in the presence of a minor by a person who resides in a home with a child, as a result of the acts or omissions of a person responsible for the care of the child

Emotional Abuse

Citation: Ann. Stat. § 232.68

The terms *child abuse* or *abuse* include any mental injury to a child's intellectual or psychological capacity as evidenced by an observable and substantial impairment in the child's ability to function within the child's normal range of performance and behavior as the result of the acts or omissions of a person responsible for the care of the child, if the impairment is diagnosed and confirmed by a licensed physician or qualified mental health professional.

Abandonment

This issue is not addressed in the statutes reviewed.

Standards for Reporting

Citation: Ann. Stat. § 232.69

A report is required when a person reasonably believes that a child has suffered abuse.

Persons Responsible for the Child

Citation: Ann. Stat. § 232.68

Person responsible for the care of a child means:

- A parent, guardian, or foster parent
- A relative or any other person with whom the child resides who assumes care or supervision of the child, without reference to the length of time or continuity of such residence
- An employee or agent of a public or private facility providing care for a child
- Any person providing care for a child but with whom the child does not reside, without reference to the duration of care

Exceptions

Citation: Ann. Stat. § 232.68

A parent or guardian legitimately practicing religious beliefs who does not provide specified medical treatment for a child for that reason alone shall not be considered abusing the child. This provision shall not preclude a court from ordering that medical service be provided to the child where the child's health requires it.

Kansas

Physical Abuse

Citation: Ann. Stat. § 38-2202

Physical, mental, or emotional abuse means the infliction of physical, mental, or emotional harm, or the causing of a deterioration of a child, and may include, but shall not be limited to, maltreatment or exploiting a child to the extent that the child's health or emotional well-being is endangered.

Neglect

Citation: Ann. Stat. § 38-2202

Neglect means acts or omissions by a parent, guardian, or person responsible for the care of a child that results in harm to a child or presents a likelihood of harm, and the acts or omissions are not due solely to the lack of financial means of the child's parents or other custodian. Neglect may include but shall not be limited to:

- Failure to provide the child with food, clothing, or shelter necessary to sustain life or health
- Failure to provide adequate supervision of a child or to remove a child from a situation that requires judgment or actions beyond the child's level of maturity, physical condition, or mental abilities and that results in bodily injury or a likelihood of harm to the child
- Failure to use resources available to treat a diagnosed medical condition if such treatment will make a child substantially more

comfortable, reduce pain and suffering, or correct or substantially diminish a crippling condition from worsening

Sexual Abuse/Exploitation

Citation: Ann. Stat. § 38-2202

Sexual abuse means any contact or interaction with a child in which the child is being used for the sexual stimulation of the perpetrator, the child, or another person. Sexual abuse includes allowing, permitting, or encouraging a child to engage in prostitution or to be photographed, filmed, or depicted in pornographic material.

Emotional Abuse

Citation: Ann. Stat. § 38-2202

The term *physical, mental, or emotional abuse* includes the infliction of physical, mental, or emotional harm or the causing of a deterioration of a child and may include, but is not limited to, maltreatment or exploiting a child to the extent that the child's health or emotional well-being is endangered.

Abandonment

Citation: Ann. Stat. § 38-2202

Abandon or *abandonment* means to forsake, desert, or cease providing care for the child without making appropriate provisions for substitute care.

Standards for Reporting

Citation: Ann. Stat. § 38-2223

A report is required when there is reason to suspect that a child has been harmed as a result of physical, mental, or emotional abuse or neglect or sexual abuse.

Persons Responsible for the Child

Citation: Ann. Stat. § 38-2202

Parent, when used in relation to a child or children, includes a guardian and every person who is by law liable to maintain, care for, or support the child.

Exceptions

Citation: Ann. Stat. § 38-2202

A parent legitimately practicing religious beliefs who does not provide specified medical treatment for a child because of religious beliefs shall not for that reason be considered a negligent parent. This exception shall not preclude a court from ordering medical treatment for the child.

Kentucky

Physical Abuse

Citation: Rev. Stat. § 600.020

Abused or neglected child means a child whose health or welfare is harmed or threatened with harm when his or her parent, guardian, or other person exercising custodial control or supervision:

- Inflicts or allows to be inflicted upon the child physical or emotional injury by other than accidental means
- Creates or allows to be created a risk of physical or emotional injury to the child by other than accidental means

Physical injury means substantial physical pain or any impairment of physical condition.

Serious physical injury means physical injury that creates a substantial risk of death, or causes serious and prolonged disfigurement, prolonged impairment of health, or prolonged loss or impairment of the function of any bodily member or organ.

Neglect

Citation: Rev. Stat. § 600.020

The term *abused or neglected child* includes a child whose health or welfare is harmed or threatened with harm when his or her parent, guardian, or other person exercising custodial control or supervision:

- Engages in a pattern of conduct that renders the parent incapable of caring for the immediate and ongoing needs of the child, including, but not limited to, parental incapacity due to alcohol and other drug abuse
- Continuously or repeatedly fails or refuses to provide essential parental care and protection for the child, considering the age of the child
- Does not provide the child with adequate care, supervision, food, clothing, shelter, education, or medical care necessary for the child's well-being
- Fails to make sufficient progress toward identified goals as set forth in the court-approved case plan to allow for the safe return of the child to the parent that results in the child remaining committed to the cabinet and remaining in foster care for 15 of the most recent 22 months

Sexual Abuse/Exploitation

Citation: Rev. Stat. § 600.020

The term *abused or neglected child* includes a child whose health or welfare is harmed or threatened with harm when his or her parent, guardian, or other person exercising custodial control or supervision:

- Commits or allows to be committed an act of sexual abuse, sexual exploitation, or prostitution upon the child
- Creates or allows to be created a risk that an act of sexual abuse, sexual exploitation, or prostitution will be committed upon the child

Sexual abuse includes, but is not necessarily limited to, any contacts or interactions in which the parent or guardian uses or allows, permits, or encourages the use of the child for the purposes of sexual stimulation of the perpetrator or another person.

Sexual exploitation includes, but is not limited to, allowing, permitting, or encouraging the child to engage in prostitution, or an act of obscene or pornographic photographing, filming, or depicting of a child.

Emotional Abuse

Citation: Rev. Stat. § 600.020

Emotional injury means an injury to the mental or psychological capacity or emotional stability of a child as evidenced by a substantial and observable impairment in the child's ability to function within a normal range of performance and behavior with due regard to his or her age, development, culture, and environment, as testified to by a qualified mental health professional.

Abandonment

Citation: Rev. Stat. § 600.020

The term *abused or neglected child* includes a child whose health or welfare is harmed or threatened with harm when his or her parent, guardian, or other person exercising custodial control or supervision abandons the child.

Standards for Reporting

Citation: Rev. Stat. § 600.030

A report is required when a person knows or has reasonable cause to believe that a child is dependent, neglected, or abused.

Persons Responsible for the Child

Citation: Rev. Stat. § 600.020

Persons responsible for the child include:

- A parent who is the biological or adoptive mother or father of a child
- A person exercising custodial control and supervision or an agency that has assumed the role and responsibility of a parent or guardian for the child but does not necessarily have legal custody of the child

Exceptions

Citation: Rev. Stat. § 600.020

A parent or other person exercising custodial control or supervision of the child who is legitimately practicing his or her religious beliefs shall not be considered a negligent parent because of failure to provide specified medical treatment for a child for that reason alone. This exception shall not preclude a court from ordering necessary medical services for a child.

Louisiana

Physical Abuse

Citation: Ch. Code art. 603

Abuse means any one of the following acts that seriously endanger the physical, mental, or emotional health and safety of the child:

- The infliction, attempted infliction, or, as a result of inadequate supervision, the allowance of the infliction or attempted infliction of physical or mental injury upon the child by a parent or any other person
- Exploitation or overwork of a child by a parent or any other person

Crime against the child means the commission or attempted commission of a crime, including homicide, battery, assault, kidnapping, criminal neglect, contributing to the delinquency or dependency of a minor, the sale of minor children, or cruelty to juveniles.

Neglect

Citation: Ch. Code art. 603

Neglect means the refusal or unreasonable failure of a parent or caregiver to supply the child with necessary food, clothing, shelter, care, treatment, or counseling for any injury, illness, or condition of the child, as a result of which the child's physical, mental, or emotional health and safety is substantially threatened or impaired. Neglect includes prenatal neglect.

Prenatal neglect means exposure to chronic or severe use of alcohol, or the unlawful use of any controlled dangerous substance or in a manner not lawfully prescribed, that results in symptoms of withdrawal in the newborn or the presence of a controlled substance or a metabolic thereof in the child's body, blood, urine, or meconium that is not the result of medical treatment; or observable and harmful effects in the child's physical appearance or functioning.

Sexual Abuse/Exploitation

Citation: Ch. Code art. 603

The term *abuse* includes any one of the following acts that seriously endanger the physical, mental, or emotional health of the child:

- The involvement of the child in any sexual act with a parent or any other person
- The aiding or toleration by the parent or caregiver of the child's sexual involvement with any other person
- The aiding or toleration by the parent of the child's involvement in pornographic displays
- Any other involvement of a child in sexual activity constituting a crime under the laws of the State

Child pornography means visual depiction of a child engaged in actual or simulated sexual intercourse, deviate sexual intercourse, sexual bestiality, masturbation, sadomasochistic abuse, or lewd exhibition of the genitals.

A *crime against a child* includes rape, sexual battery, incest, carnal knowledge of a juvenile, indecent behavior with a juvenile, pornography involving juveniles, a crime against nature, or molestation of a juvenile.

Emotional Abuse

Citation: Ch. Code art. 603

The term *abuse* includes any act that seriously endangers the mental or emotional health of the child or inflicts mental injury.

Abandonment

Citation: Ch. Code art. 603

A *crime against the child* includes criminal abandonment of a child.

Standards for Reporting

Citation: Ch. Code art. 609

A report is required when there is cause to believe that a child's physical or mental health or welfare is endangered as a result of abuse or neglect.

Persons Responsible for the Child

Citation: Ch. Code art. 603

The term *caretaker* [caregiver] means any person legally obligated to provide or secure adequate care for a child, including a parent, tutor, guardian, legal custodian, foster home parent, an employee of a public or private daycare center, operator or employee of a family daycare home, or other person providing a residence for the child.

Exceptions

Citation: Ch. Code art. 603

The inability of a parent or caregiver to provide for a child due to inadequate financial resources shall not, for that reason alone, be considered neglect.

Whenever, in lieu of medical care, a child is being provided treatment in accordance with the tenets of a well-recognized religious method of healing that has a reasonable, proven record of success, the child shall not, for that reason alone, be considered to be neglected or maltreated. Nothing in this section shall prohibit the court from ordering medical services for the child when there is substantial risk of harm to the child's health or welfare.

Maine

Physical Abuse

Citation: Ann. Stat. Tit. 22, § 4002

Abuse or neglect means a threat to a child's health or welfare by physical, mental, or emotional injury or impairment, sexual abuse or exploitation, deprivation of essential needs, or lack of protection from these, or failure to ensure compliance with school attendance requirements under Title 20-A, § 3272(2)(B), or § 5051-A(1)(C), by a person responsible for the child.

Jeopardy to health or welfare or *jeopardy* means serious abuse or neglect, as evidenced by serious harm or threat of serious harm.

Serious harm means serious injury. Serious injury means serious physical injury or impairment.

Neglect

Citation: Ann. Stat. Tit. 22, § 4002

Abuse or neglect means a threat to a child's health or welfare by deprivation of essential needs or lack of protection by a person responsible for the child.

Jeopardy to health or welfare or *jeopardy* means serious abuse or neglect, as evidenced by:

- Deprivation of adequate food, clothing, shelter, supervision, care, or education when the child is at least age 7 and has not completed grade 6
- Deprivation of necessary health care when the deprivation places the child in danger of serious harm
- Abandonment of the child or absence of any person responsible for the child that creates a threat of serious harm
- The end of voluntary placement, when the imminent return of the child to his or her custodian causes a threat of serious harm

Sexual Abuse/Exploitation

Citation: Ann. Stat. Tit. 22, § 4002

The term *abuse or neglect* includes a threat to a child's health or welfare by sexual abuse or exploitation by a person responsible for the child.

Serious harm includes sexual abuse or exploitation.

Emotional Abuse

Citation: Ann. Stat. Tit. 22, § 4002

The term *abuse or neglect* includes a threat to a child's health or welfare by mental or emotional injury or impairment by a person responsible for the child.

Serious harm includes serious mental or emotional injury or impairment that now or in the future is likely to be evidenced by serious mental, behavioral, or personality disorder, including severe anxiety, depression, withdrawal, untoward aggressive behavior, seriously delayed development, or similar serious dysfunctional behavior.

Abandonment

Citation: Ann. Stat. Tit. 22, § 4002

Abandonment means any conduct on the part of the parent that shows an intent to forgo parental duties or relinquish parental claims. The intent may be evidenced by:

- Failure to communicate meaningfully or to maintain regular visitation with the child for a period of at least 6 months
- Failure to participate in any plan or program designed to reunite the parent with the child
- Deserting the child without affording means of identifying the child and his or her parent or custodian
- Failure to respond to notice of child protective proceedings
- Any other conduct indicating an intent to forgo parental duties or relinquish parental claims

Jeopardy to health or welfare or *jeopardy* includes abandonment of the child or absence of any person responsible for the child that creates a threat of serious harm.

Standards for Reporting

Citation: Ann. Stat. Tit. 22, § 4011-A

A report is required when a person knows or has reasonable cause to suspect that a child has been or is likely to be abused or neglected.

Persons Responsible for the Child

Citation: Ann. Stat. Tit. 22, § 4002

The term *parent* means a natural or adoptive parent, unless parental rights have been terminated.

A *person responsible for the child* means a person with responsibility for a child's health or welfare, whether in the child's home or another home or facility that, as part of its function, provides for care of the child. This includes the child's custodian.

Exceptions

Citation: Ann. Stat. Tit. 22, § 4010

A child shall not be considered to be abused or neglected, in jeopardy of health or welfare, or in danger of serious harm solely because treatment is by spiritual means by an accredited practitioner of a recognized religious organization.

Maryland

Physical Abuse

Citation: Fam. Law § 5-701

Abuse means:

- The physical or mental injury of a child by any parent or other person who has permanent or temporary care, custody, or responsibility for supervision of a child, or by any household or family member, under circumstances that indicate that the child's health or welfare is harmed or at substantial risk of being harmed

- Sexual abuse of a child, whether physical injuries are sustained or not

Neglect

Citation: Fam. Law § 5-701

Neglect means the leaving of a child unattended or other failure to give proper care and attention to a child by any parent or other person who has permanent or temporary care or custody or responsibility for supervision of the child under circumstances that indicate:

- That the child's health or welfare is harmed or placed at substantial risk of harm
- Mental injury to the child or a substantial risk of mental injury

Sexual Abuse/Exploitation

Citation: Fam. Law § 5-701

Sexual abuse means any act that involves sexual molestation or exploitation of a child by a parent or other person who has permanent or temporary care, custody, or responsibility for supervision of a child, or by any household or family member. Sexual abuse includes incest, rape, sexual offense in any degree, sodomy, and unnatural or perverted sexual practices.

Emotional Abuse

Citation: Fam. Law § 5-701

Mental injury means the observable, identifiable, and substantial impairment of a child's mental or psychological ability to function.

Abandonment

This issue is not addressed in the statutes reviewed.

Standards for Reporting

Citation: Fam. Law § 5-704

A report is required when a person has reason to believe that a child has been subjected to abuse or neglect.

Persons Responsible for the Child

Citation: Fam. Law § 5-701

Responsible persons include a parent or other person who provides temporary care, custody, or supervision of the child, including:

- A *family member,* including a relative to the child by blood, adoption, or marriage
- A *household member,* including a person who lives or is a regular presence in a home of a child at the time of the alleged abuse or neglect

Exceptions

No exceptions are specified in statute.

Massachusetts

Physical Abuse

Citation: Code of Mass. Regs. Tit. 110, § 2.00

Abuse means the nonaccidental commission of any act by a caregiver upon a child under age 18 that causes or creates a substantial risk of physical or emotional injury, or constitutes a sexual offense under the laws of the Commonwealth, or any sexual contact between a caregiver and a child under the care of that individual.

- Physical injury means:
- Death
- Fracture of a bone, a subdural hematoma, burns, impairment of any organ, and any other such nontrivial injury

- Soft tissue swelling or skin bruising depending upon such factors as the child's age, circumstances under which the injury occurred, and the number and location of bruises
- Addiction to a drug at birth
- Failure to thrive

Neglect

Citation: Code of Mass. Regs. Tit. 110, § 2.00

Neglect means failure by a caregiver, either deliberately or through negligence or inability, to take those actions necessary to provide a child with minimally adequate food, clothing, shelter, medical care, supervision, emotional stability, and growth, or other essential care.

Sexual Abuse/Exploitation

Citation: Code of Mass. Regs. Tit. 110, § 2.00

The term *abuse* includes a sexual offense under the laws of the Commonwealth or any sexual contact between a caregiver and a child under the care of that individual.

Emotional Abuse

Citation: Code of Mass. Regs. Tit. 110, § 2.00

Emotional injury means an impairment to or disorder of the intellectual or psychological capacity of a child as evidenced by observable and substantial reduction in the child's ability to function within a normal range of performance and behavior.

Abandonment

Citation: Ann. Laws Ch. 119, § 39

Abandonment of an infant under age 10 occurs when:

- A person leaves the child within or without any building.
- A parent or other person who has a legal duty to care for the child, having made a contract for the child's board or maintenance, absconds or fails to perform such contract, and for 4 weeks after such

absconding or breach of contract, if of sufficient physical and mental ability, neglects to visit or remove the child or notify the department of his or her inability to support the child.

Standards for Reporting

Citation: Ann. Laws Ch. 119, § 51A

A report is required when there is reasonable cause to believe that a child is suffering from harm or substantial risk of harm resulting from abuse or neglect.

Persons Responsible for the Child

Citation: Ann. Laws Ch. 119, § 51 A; Code of Mass. Regs. Tit. 110, § 2.00

Responsible persons include the parent and any other person responsible for the child's care.

The term *caretaker* [caregiver] means:

- A child's parent, stepparent, or guardian
- Any household member entrusted with the responsibility for a child's health or welfare
- Any other person entrusted with the responsibility for a child's health or welfare whether in the child's home, a relative's home, a school setting, a daycare setting (including babysitting), a foster home, a group care facility, or any other comparable setting

Caretaker includes, but is not limited to, schoolteachers, babysitters, schoolbus drivers, camp counselors, etc.

Exceptions

Citation: Code of Mass. Regs. Tit. 110, § 2.00

It is not considered neglect when the inability to care for the child is due solely to inadequate economic resources or solely to the existence of a handicapping condition.

Michigan

Physical Abuse

Citation: Comp. Laws §§ 722.622; 722.628(3)(c)

Child abuse means harm or threatened harm to a child's health or welfare that occurs through nonaccidental physical or mental injury, sexual abuse, sexual exploitation, or maltreatment by a parent, a legal guardian, or any other person responsible for the child's health or welfare or by a teacher, a teacher's aide, or a member of the clergy.

Severe physical injury means an injury to the child that requires medical treatment or hospitalization and that seriously impairs the child's health or physical well-being.

Neglect

Citation: Comp. Laws § 722.622

Child neglect means harm or threatened harm to a child's health or welfare, by a parent, legal guardian, or any other person responsible for the child's health or welfare, that occurs through either of the following:

- Negligent treatment, including the failure to provide adequate food, clothing, shelter, or medical care
- Placing a child at an unreasonable risk to the child's health or welfare by failure to intervene to eliminate that risk when that person is able to do so and has, or should have, knowledge of the risk

Sexual Abuse/Exploitation

Citation: Comp. Laws § 722.622

Sexual abuse means engaging in sexual contact or sexual penetration with a child as those terms are defined in the penal code.

Sexual exploitation includes allowing, permitting, or encouraging a child to engage in prostitution, or allowing, permitting, encouraging, or engaging in photographing, filming, or depicting a child engaged in a sexual act.

Emotional Abuse

Citation: Comp. Laws § 722.622

The term child abuse includes mental injury.

Abandonment

This issue is not addressed in the statutes reviewed.

Standards for Reporting

Citation: Comp. Laws § 722.623

A report is required when there is reasonable cause to suspect child abuse or neglect.

Persons Responsible for the Child

Citation: Comp. Laws § 722.622

A *person responsible for the child's health* or welfare means a parent, legal guardian, person age 18 or older who resides for any length of time in the same home as the child, nonparent adult, or an owner, operator, volunteer, or employee of one or more of the following:

- A licensed or registered child care organization
- A licensed or unlicensed adult foster care family home or adult foster care small group home

Nonparent adult means a person who is age 18 or older and who, regardless of the person's domicile, meets all of the following criteria in relation to a child:

- Has substantial and regular contact with the child
- Has a close personal relationship with the child's parent or with a person responsible for the child's health or welfare
- Is not the child's parent or a person otherwise related to the child by blood or affinity to the third degree

Exceptions

Citation: Comp. Laws § 722.634

A parent or guardian legitimately practicing his or her religious beliefs who thereby does not provide specified medical treatment for a child, for that reason alone shall not be considered a negligent parent or guardian. This section shall not preclude a court from ordering the provision of medical services or nonmedical remedial services recognized by State law to a child when the child's health requires it, nor does it abrogate the responsibility of a person required to report child abuse or neglect.

Minnesota

Physical Abuse

Citation: Ann. Stat. § 626.556, Subd. 2

Physical abuse means any physical injury, mental injury, or threatened injury inflicted by a person responsible for the child's care on a child by other than accidental means, or physical or mental injury that cannot reasonably be explained by the child's history of injuries, or any aversive and deprivation procedures or regulated interventions that have not been authorized by law. Physical abuse includes, but is not limited to, any of the following acts that are done in anger or without regard to the safety of the child:

- Throwing, kicking, burning, biting, or cutting a child
- Striking a child with a closed fist
- Shaking a child under age 3
- Striking or other actions that result in any nonaccidental injury to a child under 18 months
- Unreasonable interference with a child's breathing
- Threatening a child with a weapon
- Striking a child under age 1 on the face or head
- Purposely giving a child poison, alcohol, or dangerous, harmful, or controlled substances that were not prescribed for the child by a practitioner, in order to control or punish the child; giving the child substances that substantially affect the child's behavior, motor coordination, or judgment or that result in sickness or internal injury;

or subjecting the child to medical procedures that would be unnecessary if the child were not exposed to the substances

- Unreasonable physical confinement or restraint not permitted by law including, but not limited to, tying, caging, or chaining

Neglect

Citation: Ann. Stat. § 626.556, Subd. 2

Neglect means the commission or omission of any of the acts specified below by other than accidental means:

- Failure by a person responsible for a child's care to supply a child with necessary food, clothing, shelter, health, medical, or other care required for the child's physical or mental health when reasonably able to do so
- Failure to protect a child from conditions or actions that seriously endanger the child's physical or mental health when reasonably able to do so, including a growth delay (also known as failure to thrive) that has been diagnosed by a physician and is due to parental neglect
- Failure to provide necessary and appropriate supervision or child care arrangements for a child after considering such factors as the child's age, mental ability, physical condition, length of absence, or environment, when the child is unable to care for his or her own basic needs or safety, or the basic needs or safety of another child in their care
- Failure to ensure that the child is educated as required by State law, which does not include a parent's refusal to provide his or her child with sympathomimetic medications
- Prenatal exposure to a controlled substance, used by the mother for a nonmedical purpose, as evidenced by withdrawal symptoms in the child at birth, results of a toxicology test performed on the mother at delivery or the child at birth, or medical effects or developmental delays during the child's first year of life that medically indicate prenatal exposure to a controlled substance
- *Medical neglect* that includes, but is not limited to, withholding medically indicated treatment from a disabled infant with a life-threatening condition

- Chronic and severe use of alcohol or a controlled substance by a parent or person responsible for the care of the child that adversely affects the child's basic needs and safety

Sexual Abuse/Exploitation

Citation: Ann. Stat. § 626.556, Subd. 2

Sexual abuse means the subjection of a child to any act that constitutes criminal sexual conduct by a person responsible for the child's care, a person who has a significant relationship to the child, or a person in a position of authority. Sexual abuse includes any act that involves a minor that constitutes a violation of prostitution offenses. Sexual abuse also includes threatened sexual abuse.

Emotional Abuse

Citation: Ann. Stat. §§ 260C.007, Subd. 15; 626.556, Subd. 2

Emotional maltreatment means the consistent, deliberate infliction of mental harm on a child by a person responsible for the child's care, that has an observable, sustained, and adverse effect on the child's physical, mental, or emotional development.

Mental injury means an injury to the psychological capacity or emotional stability of a child as evidenced by an observable or substantial impairment in the child's ability to function within a normal range of performance and behavior with due regard to the child's culture.

Neglect includes emotional harm from a pattern of behavior that contributes to impaired emotional functioning of the child that may be demonstrated by a substantial and observable effect in the child's behavior, emotional response, or cognition that is not within the normal range for the child's age and stage of development, with due regard to the child's culture.

Abandonment

Citation: Ann. Stat. § 260C.007, Subd. 6

Child in need of protection or services means a child who is in need of protection or services because he or she is abandoned or without a parent, guardian, or custodian.

Standards for Reporting

Citation: Ann. Stat. § 626.556, Subd. 3

A report is required when a person knows or has reason to believe that a child is neglected or physically or sexually abused.

Persons Responsible for the Child

Citation: Ann. Stat. §§ 626.556, Subd. 2; 260C.007, Subd. 15

Person responsible for the child's care means:

- An individual functioning within the family unit and having responsibilities for the care of the child such as a parent, guardian, or other person having similar care responsibilities
- An individual functioning outside the family unit and having responsibilities for the care of the child such as a teacher, school administrator, other school employees or agents, or other lawful custodian of a child having either full-time or short-term care responsibilities including, but not limited to, daycare, babysitting (paid or unpaid), counseling, teaching, and coaching

Exceptions

Citation: Ann. Stat. §§ 626.556, Subd. 2; 260C.007, Subd. 15

A child is not considered neglected solely because the child's parent, guardian, or other person responsible for the child's care in good faith selects and depends upon spiritual means or prayer for treatment or care of disease or remedial care of the child in lieu of medical care. A parent, guardian, caregiver, or a person mandated to report [child abuse or neglect] has a duty to report if a lack of medical care may cause serious danger to the child's health.

Abuse does not include reasonable and moderate physical discipline of a child administered by a parent or legal guardian that does not result in an injury.

Abuse does not include the use of reasonable force by a teacher, principal, or school employee as allowed by § 121A.582.

Emotional maltreatment does not include reasonable training or discipline administered by the person responsible for the child's care or the reasonable exercise of authority by that person.

Mississippi

Physical Abuse

Citation: Ann. Code § 43-21-105

Abused child means a child whose parent, guardian, custodian, or any person responsible for his or her care or support, whether or not legally obligated to do so, has caused or allowed to be caused upon the child nonaccidental physical injury or other maltreatment.

Neglect

Citation: Ann. Code § 43-21-105

Neglected child means a child:

- Whose parent, guardian, custodian, or any person responsible for his or her care or support neglects or refuses, when able to do so, to provide proper and necessary care or support; education as required by law; or medical, surgical, or other care necessary for his or her well-being
- Who is otherwise without proper care, custody, supervision, or support
- Who, for any reason, lacks the special care made necessary for him or her by reason of his or her mental condition, whether said mental condition be mentally retarded or mentally ill
- Who, for any reason, lacks the care necessary for his or her health, morals, or well-being

Sexual Abuse/Exploitation

Citation: Ann. Code § 43-21-105

The term *abused child* includes sexual abuse or sexual exploitation.

Sexual abuse means obscene or pornographic photographing, filming, or depiction of children for commercial purposes, or the rape, molestation, incest, prostitution, or other such forms of sexual exploitation of children under circumstances that indicate that the child's health or welfare is harmed or threatened.

Emotional Abuse

Citation: Ann. Code § 43-21-105

The term *abused child* includes emotional abuse or mental injury.

Abandonment

This issue is not addressed in the statutes reviewed.

Standards for Reporting

Citation: Ann. Code § 43-21 -353

A report is required when a person has reasonable cause to suspect that a child is abused or neglected.

Persons Responsible for the Child

Citation: Ann. Code § 43-21-105

Responsible persons include:

- A parent, guardian, or custodian
- *Any person responsible for care or support,* which refers to the person who is providing for the child at a given time, including, but not limited to, stepparents, foster parents, relatives, nonlicensed babysitters or other similar persons responsible for a child, and staff of residential care facilities and group homes licensed by the department

Exceptions

Citation: Ann. Code § 43-21-105

A parent who withholds medical treatment from any child who in good faith is under treatment by spiritual means alone through prayer, in accordance with the tenets and practices of a recognized church or religious denomination by a duly accredited practitioner thereof, shall not, for that reason alone, be considered to be neglectful.

Physical discipline, including spanking, performed on a child by a parent, guardian, or custodian in a reasonable manner shall not be deemed abuse under this section.

Missouri

Physical Abuse

Citation: Ann. Stat. § 210.110

Abuse means any physical injury inflicted on a child by other than accidental means by those responsible for the child's care, custody, and control.

Neglect

Citation: Ann. Stat. § 210.110

Neglect means failure to provide, by those responsible for the care, custody, and control of the child, proper or necessary support; education as required by law; nutrition; or medical, surgical, or any other care necessary for the child's well-being.

Sexual Abuse/Exploitation

Citation: Ann. Stat. § 210.110

The term *abuse* includes sexual abuse.

Emotional Abuse

Citation: Ann. Stat. § 210.110

The term *abuse* includes emotional abuse inflicted on a child by those responsible for the child's care, custody, and control.

Abandonment

This issue is not addressed in the statutes reviewed.

Standards for Reporting

Citation: Ann. Stat. § 210.115

A report is required when there is reasonable cause to suspect that a child has been or may be subjected to abuse or neglect.

Persons Responsible for the Child

Citation: Ann. Stat. § 210.110

The term *those responsible for the care, custody, and control of the child* includes, but is not limited to:

- The parents or guardian of a child
- Other members of the child's household
- Anyone exercising supervision over a child for any part of a 24-hour day
- Any adult who has access to the child, based on a relationship to the parents of the child, members of the child's household, or the family

Exceptions

Citation: Ann. Stat. §§ 210.110; 210.115

Discipline, including spanking, administered in a reasonable manner, shall not be considered abuse.

A child who does not receive specified medical treatment by reason of the legitimate practice of the religious belief of the child's parents, guardian, or others legally responsible for the child, for that reason alone, shall not be found to be an abused or neglected child.

- The division may accept reports concerning such a child and may subsequently investigate or conduct a family assessment as a result of that report.
- This exception shall not limit the administrative or judicial authority of the State to ensure that medical services are provided to the child when the child's health requires it.

Montana

Physical Abuse

Citation: Ann. Code § 41-3-102

Physical abuse means an intentional act, omission, or gross negligence resulting in substantial skin bruising, internal bleeding, substantial injury to skin, subdural hematoma, burns, bone fractures, extreme pain, permanent or temporary disfigurement, impairment of any bodily organ or function, or death.

Child abuse or neglect means:

- Actual physical or psychological harm to a child
- Substantial risk of physical or psychological harm to a child
- Abandonment

The term includes:

- Actual physical or psychological harm to a child, or substantial risk of physical or psychological harm to a child, by the acts or omissions of a person responsible for the child's welfare
- Exposing a child to the criminal distribution of dangerous drugs, the criminal production or manufacture of dangerous drugs, or the operation of an unlawful clandestine laboratory

Physical or psychological harm to a child means the harm that occurs whenever the parent or other person responsible for the child's welfare inflicts or allows to be inflicted upon the child physical abuse, physical neglect, or psychological abuse or neglect.

Neglect

Citation: Ann. Code § 41-3-102

Physical neglect means:

- Failure to provide basic necessities, including but not limited to appropriate and adequate nutrition, protective shelter from the elements, and appropriate clothing related to weather conditions
- Failure to provide cleanliness and general supervision
- Exposing or allowing the child to be exposed to an unreasonable physical or psychological risk to the child

Physical or psychological harm to a child means the harm that occurs whenever the parent or other person responsible for the child's welfare:

- Causes malnutrition, failure to thrive, or otherwise fails to supply the child with adequate food; fails to supply clothing, shelter, education, or adequate health care, though financially able to do so or when offered financial or other reasonable means to do so
- Exposes the child, or allows the child to be exposed, to an unreasonable risk to the child's health or welfae by failing to intervene or eliminate the risk

Withholding of medically indicated treatment means failure to respond to an infant's life-threatening conditions by not providing treatment, including appropriate nutrition, hydration, and medication, that in the treating physician's or physicians' reasonable medical judgment is most likely to be effective in ameliorating or correcting the conditions.

Sexual Abuse/Exploitation

Citation: Ann. Code § 41-3-102

Sexual abuse means the commission of sexual assault, sexual intercourse without consent, indecent exposure, deviate sexual conduct, ritual abuse, or incest.

Sexual exploitation means allowing, permitting, or encouraging a child to engage in a prostitution offense or allowing, permitting, or encouraging sexual abuse of children.

Physical or psychological harm to a child means the harm that occurs whenever a parent or other person responsible for the child's welfare commits or allows sexual abuse or exploitation of the child.

Emotional Abuse

Citation: Ann. Code § 41-3-102

Psychological abuse or neglect means severe maltreatment through acts or omissions that are injurious to the child's emotional, intellectual, or psychological capacity to function, including acts of violence against another person residing in the child's home.

Physical or psychological harm to a child means the harm that occurs whenever a parent or other person responsible for a child's welfare induces or attempts to induce the child to give untrue testimony that the child or another child was abused or neglected by a parent or other person responsible for the child's welfare.

Abandonment

Citation: Ann. Code § 41-3-102

Abandon, abandoned, and *abandonment* mean:

- Leaving a child under circumstances that make reasonable the belief that the parent does not intend to resume care of the child in the future
- Willfully surrendering physical custody for a period of 6 months and during that period not manifesting to the child and the person having physical custody of the child a firm intention to resume physical custody or to make permanent legal arrangements for the care of the child
- That the parent is unknown and has been unknown for a period of 90 days and that reasonable efforts to identify and locate the parent have failed
- The voluntary surrender, as defined in § 40-6-402, by a parent of a newborn who is no more than 30 days old to an emergency services provider

Physical or psychological harm to a child means the harm that occurs when the parent or other person responsible for the child's welfare abandons the child.

Standards for Reporting

Citation: Ann. Code § 41-3-201

A report is required when there is reasonable cause to suspect that a child is abused or neglected.

Persons Responsible for the Child

Citation: Ann. Code § 41-3-102

A person responsible for a child's welfare means:

- The child's parent, guardian, foster parent, or an adult who resides in the same home as the child
- A person providing care in a daycare facility

- An employee of a public or private residential institution, facility, home, or agency
- Any other person responsible for the child's welfare in a residential setting

Exceptions

Citation: Ann. Code § 41-3-102

The term *abandoned* does not include the voluntary surrender of the child to the department solely because of parental inability to access publicly funded services.

The term *child abuse* does not include self-defense, defense of others, or action taken to prevent the child from self- harm.

This chapter may not be construed to require or justify a finding of child abuse or neglect for the sole reason that a parent or legal guardian, because of religious beliefs, does not provide adequate health care for a child. This chapter may not be construed to limit the administrative or judicial authority of the State to ensure that medical care is provided to the child when there is imminent substantial risk of serious harm to the child.

The term *withholding medically indicated treatment* does not include the failure to provide treatment, other than appropriate nutrition, hydration, or medication to an infant when, in the treating physician's or physicians' reasonable medical judgment:

- The infant is chronically and irreversibly comatose.
- The provision of treatment would merely prolong dying, not be effective in ameliorating or correcting all of the infant's life-threatening conditions, or otherwise be futile in terms of the survival of the infant.
- The provision of treatment would be virtually futile in terms of the survival of the infant, and the treatment itself under the circumstances would be inhumane.

Nebraska

Physical Abuse

Citation: Rev. Stat. § 28-710

Child abuse or neglect means knowingly, intentionally, or negligently causing, or permitting a minor child to be placed in a situation that endangers his or her life or physical health, or causes or permits a child to be cruelly confined or cruelly punished.

Neglect

Citation: Rev. Stat. § 28-710

Child abuse or neglect means knowingly, intentionally, or negligently causing or permitting a minor child to be deprived of necessary food, clothing, shelter, or care or causing or permitting a child age 6 or younger to be left unattended in a motor vehicle.

Sexual Abuse/Exploitation

Citation: Rev. Stat. § 28-710

The term *child abuse or neglect* includes knowingly, intentionally, or negligently causing or permitting a minor child to be:

- Sexually abused
- Sexually exploited by allowing, encouraging, or forcing the child to solicit for or engage in prostitution, debauchery, public indecency, or obscene or pornographic photography, films, or depictions

Emotional Abuse

Citation: Rev. Stat. § 28-710

The term *child abuse or neglect* includes knowingly, intentionally, or negligently causing or permitting a minor child to be placed in a situation that endangers his or her mental health.

Abandonment

Citation: Rev. Stat. § 28-705(3)

When a person abandons and neglects to provide for his or her child or dependent stepchild for 3 consecutive months or more, it shall be *prima facie* evidence of intent to commit abandonment of a child or dependent stepchild.

Standards for Reporting

Citation: Rev. Stat. § 28-711

A report is required when there is reasonable cause to believe that a child has been subjected to abuse or neglect.

Persons Responsible for the Child

Citation: Rev. Stat. § 28-710

A report must be made when any person is responsible for the abuse or neglect of a child.

Exceptions

No exceptions are specified in statute.

Nevada

Physical Abuse

Citation: Rev. Stat. §§ 432B.020; 432B.090; 432B.150

Abuse or neglect of a child means physical or mental injury of a nonaccidental nature; sexual abuse or sexual exploitation; or negligent treatment or maltreatment of a child caused or allowed by a person responsible for his or her welfare under circumstances that indicate that the child's health or welfare is harmed or threatened with harm.

Physical injury includes, without limitation:

- A sprain or dislocation
- Damage to cartilage
- A fracture of a bone or the skull

- An intracranial hemorrhage or injury to another internal organ
- A burn or scalding
- A cut, laceration, puncture, or bite
- Permanent or temporary disfigurement or loss or impairment of a part or organ of the body

Excessive corporal punishment may result in physical or mental injury constituting abuse or neglect of a child.

Neglect

Citation: Rev. Stat. § 432B.140

Negligent treatment or maltreatment of a child occurs if a child has been abandoned; is without proper care, control, and supervision; or lacks the subsistence, education, shelter, medical care, or other care necessary for the well-being of the child because of the faults or habits of the person responsible for his or her welfare or because of that person's neglect or refusal to provide care when able to do so.

Sexual Abuse/Exploitation

Citation: Rev. Stat. §§ 432B.100; 432B.110

Sexual abuse includes acts upon a child constituting:

- Incest
- Lewdness with a child
- Sadomasochistic abuse
- Sexual assault
- Statutory sexual seduction
- Mutilation of the genitalia of a female child; aiding, abetting, encouraging, or participating in the mutilation of the genitalia of a female child; or removal of a female child from this State for the purpose of mutilating the genitalia of the child

Sexual exploitation includes forcing, allowing, or encouraging a child:

- To solicit for or engage in prostitution
- To view a pornographic film or literature

- To engage in filming, photographing, recording on videotape, posing, modeling, depiction, or a live performance before an audience that involves the exhibition of a child's genitals or any sexual conduct with a child

Emotional Abuse

Citation: Rev. Stat. § 432B.070

Mental injury means an injury to the intellectual or psychological capacity or the emotional condition of a child as evidenced by an observable and substantial impairment of his or her ability to function within his or her normal range of performance or behavior.

Abandonment

Citation: Rev. Stat. § 432B.140

Negligent treatment or maltreatment of a child occurs if a child has been abandoned.

Standards for Reporting

Citation: Rev. Stat. § 432B.220

A report is required when a person knows or has reasonable cause to believe that a child has been abused or neglected.

Persons Responsible for the Child

Citation: Rev. Stat. §§ 432B.080; 432B.130

The term *parent* means a natural or adoptive parent whose parental rights have not been terminated.

The term *person responsible for a child's welfare* includes:

- The child's parent, guardian, or stepparent with whom the child lives
- An adult person continually or regularly found in the same household as the child
- A person directly responsible, serving as a volunteer, or employed in a public or private home, institution, or facility where a child actually

resides or is receiving child care outside his or her home for a portion of the day

Exceptions

Citation: Rev. Stat. § 432B.020(2)

Relinquishment of a newborn in accordance with the law is not considered abuse or neglect.

It is not considered abuse or neglect when a parent or guardian, in good faith, selects and depends upon nonmedical remedial treatment for the child, if such treatment is recognized and permitted under the laws of the State in lieu of medical treatment. This paragraph does not limit the court in ensuring that a child receive a medical examination and treatment pursuant to § 62E.280.

New Hampshire

Physical Abuse

Citation: Rev. Stat. § 1 69-C:3

Abused child means any child who has been:

- Sexually abused
- Intentionally physically injured
- Physically injured by other than accidental means

Neglect

Citation: Rev. Stat. § 1 69-C:3

Neglected child means a child:

- Who is without proper parental care or control, subsistence, education as required by law, or other care or control necessary for his or her physical, mental, or emotional health, when it is established that his or her health has suffered or is very likely to suffer serious impairment, and the deprivation is not due primarily to the lack of financial means of the parents, guardian, or custodian

- Whose parents, guardian, or custodian are unable to discharge their responsibilities to and for the child because of incarceration, hospitalization, or other physical or mental incapacity

Sexual Abuse/Exploitation

Citation: Rev. Stat. § 1 69-C:3

Sexual abuse means the following activities under circumstances that indicate that the child's health or welfare is harmed or threatened with harm:

- The employment, use, persuasion, inducement, enticement, or coercion of any child to engage in or having a child assist any other person to engage in any sexually explicit conduct or any simulation of such conduct for the purpose of producing any visual depiction of such conduct
- The rape, molestation, prostitution, or other form of sexual exploitation of children, or incest with children

Emotional Abuse

Citation: Rev. Stat. § 1 69-C:3

The term *abused child* includes any child who has been psychologically injured so that the child exhibits symptoms of emotional problems generally recognized to result from consistent mistreatment or neglect.

Abandonment

Citation: Rev. Stat. § 1 69-C:3

Abandoned means the child has been left by his or her parent, guardian, or custodian without provision for his or her care, supervision, or financial support, although his or her parent, guardian, or custodian is financially able to provide such support.

Standards for Reporting

Citation: Rev. Stat. § 1 69-C:329

A report is required when there is reason to suspect that a child has been abused or neglected.

Persons Responsible for the Child

Citation: Rev. Stat. § 1 69-C:3

A person responsible for a child's welfare includes the child's parent, guardian, or custodian, as well as the person providing out-of-home care of the child, if that person is not the parent, guardian, or custodian.

The term *parent* means mother, father, or adoptive parent, but the term shall not include a parent whose parent-child relationship has been terminated by judicial decree or voluntary relinquishment.

Exceptions

Citation: Rev. Stat. § 1 69-C:3

No child who is, in good faith, under treatment solely by spiritual means through prayer in accordance with the tenets and practices of a recognized church or religious denomination by a duly accredited practitioner thereof shall, for that reason alone, be considered to be a neglected child under this chapter.

New Jersey

Physical Abuse

Citation: Ann. Stat. § 9:6-8.21

Abused child or *abused or neglected child* means a child under age 18 whose parent, guardian, or other person having custody and control:

- Inflicts or allows to be inflicted upon such child physical injury by other than accidental means that causes or creates a substantial risk of death, serious or protracted disfigurement, protracted impairment of physical or emotional health, or protracted loss or impairment of the function of any bodily organ
- Creates or allows to be created a substantial or ongoing risk of physical injury to such child by other than accidental means
- Unreasonably inflicts, or allows to be inflicted, harm or substantial risk thereof, including the infliction of excessive corporal punishment

or by any other acts of a similarly serious nature requiring the aid of the court

- Uses excessive physical restraint upon the child under circumstances that do not indicate that the child's behavior is harmful to himself, others, or property

Neglect

Citation: Ann. Stat. § 9:6-8.21

Abused child or *abused or neglected child* means a child younger than age 18 whose physical, mental, or emotional condition has been impaired or is in imminent danger of becoming impaired as the result of the failure of his parent, guardian, or other person having custody and control, to exercise a minimum degree of care:

- In supplying the child with adequate food, clothing, shelter, education, medical, or surgical care, although financially able to do so or although offered financial or other reasonable means to do so
- In providing the child with proper supervision or guardianship

Sexual Abuse/Exploitation

Citation: Ann. Stat. § 9:6-8.21

The terms *abused child* or *abused or neglected child* include a child under age 18 whose parent, guardian, or other person having custody and control commits or allows to be committed an act of sexual abuse against the child.

Emotional Abuse

Citation: Ann. Stat. § 9:6-8.21

The terms *abused child* or *abused or neglected child* include a child under age 18 who is in an institution, and:

- Has been placed there inappropriately for a continued period of time with the knowledge that the placement has resulted or may continue to result in harm to the child's mental or physical well-being
- Who has been willfully isolated from ordinary social contact under circumstances that indicate emotional or social deprivation

Abandonment

Citation: Ann. Stat. § 9:6-8.21

The terms *abused child* or *abused or neglected child* include a child under age 18 who has been willfully abandoned by his or her parent, guardian, or other person having custody and control.

Standards for Reporting

Citation: Ann. Stat. § 9:6-8.10

A report is required when there is reasonable cause to believe that a child has been subjected to child abuse.

Persons Responsible for the Child

Citation: Ann. Stat. § 9:6-8.21

Parent or guardian means any natural parent, adoptive parent, resource family parent, stepparent, paramour of a parent, or any person who has assumed responsibility for the care, custody, or control of a child or upon whom there is a legal duty for such care.

Parent or guardian includes a teacher, employee, or volunteer, whether compensated or uncompensated, of an institution who is responsible for the child's welfare and any other staff person of an institution, regardless of whether or not the person is responsible for the care or supervision of the child. Parent or guardian also includes a teaching staff member or other employee, whether compensated or uncompensated, of a day school.

Exceptions

Citation: Ann. Stat. § 9:6-8.21

No child who in good faith is under treatment by spiritual means alone through prayer in accordance with the tenets and practices of a recognized church or religious denomination by a duly accredited practitioner thereof shall for this reason alone be considered to be abused or neglected.

New Mexico

Physical Abuse

Citation: Ann. Stat. § 32A-4-2

Abused child means a child:

- Who has suffered or is at risk of suffering serious harm because of the action or inaction of the child's parent, guardian, or custodian
- Who has suffered physical abuse inflicted or caused by the child's parent, guardian, or custodian
- Whose parent, guardian, or custodian has knowingly, intentionally, or negligently placed the child in a situation that may endanger the child's life or health
- Whose parent, guardian, or custodian has knowingly or intentionally tortured, cruelly confined, or cruelly punished the child

Physical abuse includes, but is not limited to, any case in which the child exhibits evidence of skin bruising, bleeding, malnutrition, failure to thrive, burns, fracture of any bone, subdural hematoma, soft tissue swelling, or death, and:

- There is no justifiable explanation for the condition or death.
- The explanation given for the condition or death is at variance with the degree or nature of the condition or the nature of the death.
- Circumstances indicate that the condition or death may not be the product of an accidental occurrence.

Neglect

Citation: Ann. Stat. § 32A-4-2

Neglected child means a child:

- Who has been abandoned by the child's parent, guardian, or custodian
- Who is without proper parental care and control or subsistence, education, medical, or other care or control necessary for the child's well-being because of the faults or habits of the child's parent,

guardian, or custodian or that person's failure or refusal to provide them

- Who has been physically or sexually abused when the child's parent, guardian, or custodian knew or should have known of the abuse and failed to take reasonable steps to protect the child from further harm
- Whose parent, guardian, or custodian is unable to discharge his or her responsibilities to and for the child because of incarceration, hospitalization, or other physical or mental disorder or incapacity
- Who has been placed for care or adoption in violation of the law

Sexual Abuse/Exploitation

Citation: Ann. Stat. § 32A-4-2

The term *abused child* includes a child who has suffered sexual abuse or sexual exploitation inflicted by the child's parent, guardian, or custodian.

Sexual abuse includes, but is not limited to, criminal sexual contact, incest, or criminal sexual penetration, as those acts are defined by State law.

Sexual exploitation includes, but is not limited to:

- Allowing, permitting, or encouraging a child to engage in prostitution
- Allowing, permitting, encouraging, or engaging a child in obscene or pornographic photographing
- Filming or depicting a child for obscene or pornographic commercial purposes

Emotional Abuse

Citation: Ann. Stat. § 32A-4-2

The term *abused child* includes a child who has suffered emotional or psychological abuse inflicted or caused by the child's parent, guardian, or custodian.

Abandonment

Citation: Ann. Stat. § 32A-4-2

Abandonment includes instances when the parent, without justifiable cause:

- Left the child without provision for the child's identification for a period of 14 days
- Left the child with others, including the other parent or an agency, without provision for support and without communication for a period of 3 months if the child was younger than age 6 at the commencement of the 3-month period or 6 months if the child was older than age 6 at the commencement of the 6-month period

Standards for Reporting

Citation: Ann. Stat. § 32A-4-3

A report is required when a person knows or has a reasonable suspicion that the child is abused or neglected.

Persons Responsible for the Child

Citation: Ann. Stat. § 32A-4-2

Responsible persons include the child's parent, guardian, or custodian.

Exceptions

Citation: Ann. Stat. § 32A-4-2

A child who is being provided with treatment by spiritual means alone through prayer, in accordance with the tenets and practices of a recognized church or religious denomination, by a duly accredited practitioner thereof is not for that reason alone a neglected child.

New York

Physical Abuse

Citation: Soc. Serv. Law § 371

Abused child means a child younger than age 18 whose parent or other person legally responsible for his or her care:

- Inflicts or allows to be inflicted upon such child physical injury by other than accidental means that causes or creates a substantial risk of death, serious or protracted disfigurement, protracted impairment of physical or emotional health, or protracted loss or impairment of the function of any bodily organ

- Creates or allows to be created a substantial risk of physical injury to such child by other than accidental means that would be likely to cause death, serious or protracted disfigurement, protracted impairment of physical or emotional health, or protracted loss or impairment of the function of any bodily organ

Neglect

Citation: Soc. Serv. Law § 371

Neglected child means a child younger than age 18 whose physical, mental, or emotional condition has been impaired or is in imminent danger of becoming impaired as a result of the failure of his or her parent or other person legally responsible for his or her care to exercise a minimum degree of care:

In supplying the child with adequate food, clothing, shelter, education, or medical or surgical care, although financially able to do so or offered financial or other reasonable means to do so

- In providing the child with proper supervision or guardianship
- By unreasonably inflicting or allowing harm to be inflicted, or a substantial risk thereof, including the infliction of excessive corporal punishment
- By misusing drugs or alcoholic beverages to the extent that he or she loses self-control of his or her actions
- By any other acts of a similarly serious nature requiring the aid of the court

Sexual Abuse/Exploitation

Citation: Soc. Serv. Law § 371

The term *abused child* includes a child younger than age 18 whose parent or other person legally responsible for his or her care commits, or allows to be committed, an act of sexual abuse against such child, as defined in title H, article 130, of the penal law.

Emotional Abuse

Citation: Family Court Act § 1012

Impairment of emotional health and impairment of mental or emotional condition includes a state of substantially diminished psychological or intellectual functioning in relation to, but not limited to, such factors as failure to thrive, control of aggressive or self-destructive impulses, ability to think and reason, acting out, or misbehavior, including incorrigibility, ungovernability, or habitual truancy; provided, however, that such impairment must be clearly attributable to the unwillingness or inability of the respondent to exercise a minimum degree of care toward the child.

Abandonment

Citation: Soc. Serv. Law § 384-b

A child is *abandoned* by his or her parent if such parent evinces an intent to forgo his or her parental rights and obligations as manifested by his or her failure to visit the child and communicate with the child or agency, although able to do so and not prevented or discouraged from doing so by the agency. In the absence of evidence to the contrary, such ability to visit and communicate shall be presumed.

Standards for Reporting

Citation: Soc. Serv. Law § 413

A report is required when there is reasonable cause to suspect that a child has been abused or maltreated.

Persons Responsible for the Child

Citation: Soc. Serv. Law § 371; Family Court Act § 1012

Responsible persons include the child's parent and other persons legally responsible for the child's care.

Person legally responsible includes the child's custodian, guardian, and any other person responsible for the child's care at the relevant time. A custodian may include a person continually or at regular intervals found in the same household as the child when the conduct of such person causes or contributes to the abuse or neglect of the child.

Exceptions

No exceptions are specified in statute.

North Carolina

Physical Abuse

Citation: Gen. Stat. § 7B-101

Abused juvenile means any child younger than age 18 whose parent, guardian, custodian, or caregiver:

- Inflicts or allows to be inflicted upon the child a serious physical injury by other than accidental means
- Creates or allows to be created a substantial risk of serious physical injury to the child by other than accidental means
- Uses or allows to be used upon the child cruel or grossly inappropriate procedures or cruel or grossly inappropriate devices to modify behavior

Neglect

Citation: Gen. Stat. § 7B-1 01

Neglected juvenile means a child:

- Who does not receive proper care, supervision, or discipline from his or her parent, guardian, custodian, or caregiver
- Who is not provided necessary medical or remedial care
- Who lives in an environment injurious to his or her welfare
- Who has been placed for care or adoption in violation of law

In determining whether a child is a neglected juvenile, it is relevant whether that child lives in a home where another child has been subjected to abuse or neglect by an adult who regularly lives in the home.

Sexual Abuse/Exploitation

Citation: Gen. Stat. § 7B-1 01

The term *abused juvenile* includes any child younger than age 18 whose parent, guardian, custodian, or caregiver commits, permits, or encourages the commission of a violation of the following laws regarding sexual offenses by, with, or upon the child:

- First and second degree rape or sexual offense
- Rape of a child by an adult offender
- Sexual act by a custodian
- Crime against nature or incest
- Preparation of obscene photographs, slides, or motion pictures of the child
- Employing or permitting the child to assist in a violation of the obscenity laws
- Dissemination of obscene material to the child
- Displaying or disseminating material harmful to the child
- First and second degree sexual exploitation of the child
- Promoting the prostitution of the child
- Taking indecent liberties with the child

Emotional Abuse

Citation: Gen. Stat. § 7B-1 01

The term *abused juvenile* includes any child younger than age 18 whose parent, guardian, custodian, or caregiver creates or allows to be created serious emotional damage to the child. Serious emotional damage is evidenced by a child's severe anxiety, depression, withdrawal, or aggressive behavior toward himself or others.

Abandonment

Citation: Gen. Stat. § 7B-1 01

The term *neglected juvenile* includes a child who has been abandoned.

Standards for Reporting

Citation: Gen. Stat. § 7B-301

A report is required when there is cause to suspect that a child is abused, neglected, or dependent.

Persons Responsible for the Child

Citation: Gen. Stat. § 7B-101

A *person responsible for a child's health and welfare* means:

- A parent, guardian, or custodian
- A stepparent, foster parent, or an adult member of the child's household
- An adult relative entrusted with the child's care
- Any person, such as a house parent or cottage parent, who has primary responsibility for supervising a child's health and welfare in a residential child care facility
- An employee or volunteer of a division, institution, or school operated by the department

Exceptions

No exceptions are specified in statute.

North Dakota

Physical Abuse

Citation: Cent. Code §§ 50-25.1 -02; 14-09-22

Abused child means an individual younger than age 18 who is suffering from abuse as defined in § 14-09-22(1)(a), caused by a person responsible for the child's welfare.

A child is abused when a parent, adult family or household member, guardian, or other custodian of any child willfully does any of the following:

- Inflicts or allows to be inflicted upon the child bodily injury, substantial bodily injury, serious bodily injury, or mental injury

- Fails to provide proper parental care or control, subsistence, education as required by law, or other care or control necessary for the child's physical, mental, or emotional health, or morals
- Permits the child to be, or fails to exercise reasonable diligence in preventing the child from being, in a disreputable place or associating with vagrants or vicious or immoral persons
- Permits the child to engage in, or fails to exercise reasonable diligence in preventing the child from engaging in, an occupation forbidden by the laws of this State or an occupation injurious to the child's health or morals, or the health or morals of others

Neglect

Citation: Cent. Code §§ 50-25.1 -02; 27-20-02

Neglected child means a deprived child as defined in chapter 27-20.

Deprived child means a child who:

- Is without proper parental care or control, subsistence, education, or other care or control necessary for the child's physical, mental, emotional health, or morals; and the deprivation is not due primarily to the lack of financial means of the child's parents, guardian, or other custodian
- Has been placed for care or adoption in violation of law
- Is without proper parental care, control, education, or other care and control necessary for the child's well-being because of the physical, mental, emotional, or other illness or disability of the child's parent or parents; and such lack of care is not due to a willful act of commission or act of omission by the child's parents, and care is requested by a parent
- Is in need of treatment and whose parents, guardian, or other custodian have refused to participate in treatment as ordered by the juvenile court
- Was subject to prenatal exposure to chronic and severe use of alcohol or any controlled substance in a manner not lawfully prescribed by a practitioner
- Is present in an environment that subjects the child to exposure to a controlled substance or drug paraphernalia

Prenatal exposure to a controlled substance means use of a controlled substance by a pregnant woman for a nonmedical purpose during pregnancy as evidenced by withdrawal symptoms in the child at birth, results of a toxicology test performed on the mother at delivery of the child at birth, or medical effects or developmental delays during the child's first year of life that medically indicate prenatal exposure to a controlled substance.

Sexual Abuse/Exploitation

Citation: Cent. Code § 50-25.1 -02

Sexually abused child means an individual younger than age 18 who is subjected by a person responsible for the child's welfare or by any individual to sexual abuse, as described in §§ 12.1-20-01 through 12.1-20-07 and §§ 12.1-20-11 through 12.1-20-12.2, or sexual exploitation, as described in chapter 12.1-27.2.

Emotional Abuse

Citation: Cent. Code § 50-25.1 -02

A child is an *abused child* when the person responsible for the child's welfare inflicts or allows to be inflicted upon the child a mental injury.

Abandonment

Citation: Cent. Code § 27-20-02

Abandon means:

- Failure by a noncustodial parent, without justifiable cause, to communicate significantly with the child, or to provide for the care and support of the child as required by law
- Actions by a custodial parent that include:
  - Leaving the child for an indefinite period without making firm and agreed upon plans with the child's immediate caregiver for the parents' resumption of physical custody
  - Following the child's birth or treatment at a hospital, failing to arrange for the child's discharge within 10 days after the child no longer requires hospital care

- Willfully failing to furnish food, shelter, clothing, or medical attention that is reasonably sufficient to meet the child's needs

Abandoned infant means a child who has been abandoned before reaching the age of 1 year.

Standards for Reporting

Citation: Cent. Code § 50-25.1-03

A report is required when a person knows or has reasonable cause to suspect that a child is abused or neglected.

Persons Responsible for the Child

Citation: Cent. Code § 50-25.1 -02

A person responsible for the child's welfare means a person who has responsibility for the care or supervision of a child and who is:

- The child's parent, an adult family member of the child, any member of the child's household, the child's guardian, or the child's foster parent
- An employee of, or any person providing care for the child in, a public or private school or child care setting

Exceptions

No exceptions are specified in statute.

Northern Mariana Islands

Physical Abuse

Citation: Commonwealth Code Tit. 6, § 5312

Child abuse is committed if the person willfully and intentionally strikes, beats, or by any other act or omission inflicts physical pain, injury, or mental distress upon a child younger than age 18 who is in the person's custody, such pain or injury being clearly beyond the scope of reasonable corporal punishment, with the result that the child's physical or mental health and well-being are harmed or threatened.

Neglect

Citation: Commonwealth Code Tit. 6, § 5312

Child abuse is committed if a person, through willful or negligent acts or omissions, fails to provide a child younger than age 18 who is in the person's custody adequate supervision, medical care, food, clothing, or shelter with the result that the child's physical or mental health and well-being are harmed or threatened.

Sexual Abuse/Exploitation

Citation: Commonwealth Code Tit. 6, §§ 1314; 5312

Child abuse is committed if the person engages in or attempts to engage in an act of sexual molestation with a child younger than age 18 who is in the person's custody.

A parent, legal guardian, or person having custody or control of a child younger than age 18 commits the crime of unlawful exploitation of a minor if the person permits the child to engage in [actual or simulated] conduct [of a sexual nature] knowing that the conduct is intended to be used in producing a live performance, film, audio, video, electronic, or electromagnetic recording, photograph, negative, slide, book, newspaper, magazine, or other material that visually or aurally depicts the conduct.

Emotional Abuse

Citation: Commonwealth Code Tit. 6, § 5312

Mental distress or injury means an effect on the intellectual or psychological capacity of a child as evidenced by observable and substantial impairment of his or her ability to function within normal ranges of performance and behavior, with due regard to his or her culture.

Abandonment

This issue is not addressed in the statutes reviewed.

Standards for Reporting

Citation: Commonwealth Code Tit. 6, § 5313

A report is required when a person knows or has reasonable cause to suspect that a child is abused or neglected.

Persons Responsible for the Child

Citation: Commonwealth Code Tit. 6, §§ 1314; 5312

Responsible persons include:

- A parent or legal guardian
- A person who has custody or control of a child

Exceptions

Citation: Commonwealth Code Tit. 6, § 5312

Child abuse does not include the exercise of reasonable and traditional parental discipline.

Ohio

Physical Abuse

Citation: Rev. Stat. §§ 2151 .031; 2919.22

Abused child includes any child who:

- Is endangered as defined § 2919.22
- Exhibits evidence of any physical or mental injury or death, inflicted by other than accidental means, that is at variance with the history given of it
- Suffers physical or mental injury that harms or threatens to harm the child's health or welfare because of the acts of his or her parent, guardian, or custodian
- Is subjected to out-of-home-care child abuse

Endangering children includes any of the following acts committed against a child under age 18 or a mentally or physically handicapped child under age 21:

- Abuse, torture, or cruel abuse
- Corporal punishment, other physical disciplinary measure, or physical restraint in a cruel manner or for a prolonged period that creates a substantial risk of serious physical harm to the child
- Repeated and unwarranted disciplinary measures that, if continued, create a substantial risk of serious impairment of the child's mental health or development
- Allowing the child to be on the same parcel of real property and within 100 feet of, or, in the case of more than one housing unit on the same parcel of real property, in the same housing unit and within 100 feet of, the illegal manufacture of drugs, cultivation of marijuana, or possession of chemicals for the illegal manufacture, when the person knows that the act is occurring, whether or not any person is prosecuted for or convicted of the violation

Neglect

Citation: Rev. Stat. § 2151.03(A)

Neglected child includes any child:

- Who lacks proper parental care because of the faults or habits of the child's parents, guardian, or custodian
- Whose parents, guardian, or custodian neglects the child or refuses to provide proper or necessary subsistence, education, medical or surgical care or treatment, or other care necessary for the child's health, morals, or wellbeing
- Whose parents, guardian, or custodian neglects the child or refuses to provide the special care made necessary by the child's mental condition
- Whose parents, legal guardian, or custodian have placed or attempted to place the child in violation of statutes regarding the placement and adoption of children
- Who, because of the omission of the child's parents, guardian, or custodian, suffers physical or mental injury that harms or threatens to harm the child's health or welfare

- Who is subjected to child neglect in out-of-home care

Sexual Abuse/Exploitation

Citation: Rev. Stat. §§ 2151.031; 2907.01; 2919.22

The term *abused child* includes a child who is the victim of sexual activity when such activity would constitute an offense, except that the court need not find that any person has been convicted of the offense in order to find that the child is an abused child. Sexual activity means sexual conduct or sexual contact or both.

Sexual conduct means vaginal intercourse between a male and female; anal intercourse, fellatio, and cunnilingus between persons regardless of sex; and, without privilege to do so, the insertion, however slight, of any part of the body of any instrument, apparatus, or other object into the vaginal or anal opening of another. Penetration, however slight, is sufficient to complete vaginal or anal intercourse.

Sexual contact means any touching of an erogenous zone of another, including without limitation, the thigh, genitals, buttocks, pubic region, and if the person is a female, a breast, for the purpose of sexually arousing or gratifying either person.

A person commits the crime of *endangering children* when the person does any of the following to a child: Entice, coerce, permit, encourage, compel, hire, employ, use, or allow the child to act, model, or in any other way participate in, or be photographed for, the production, presentation, dissemination, or advertisement of any material or performance that the offender knows or reasonably should know is obscene, sexually oriented, or nudity-oriented matter.

Emotional Abuse

Citation: Rev. Stat. § 2151.011

Mental injury means any behavioral, cognitive, emotional, or mental disorder in a child caused by an act or omission that is described in § 2919.22 and is committed by a parent or other person who is responsible for the child's care.

Abandonment

Citation: Rev. Stat. §§ 2151 .03(A); 2151.011

The term *neglected child* includes a child who is abandoned by his or her parents, guardian, or custodian.

A child shall be presumed abandoned when his or her parents have failed to visit or maintain contact with him or her for more than 90 days, regardless of whether the parents resume contact with the child after that period of 90 days.

Standards for Reporting

Citation: Rev. Stat, § 2151.421

A report is required when a person knows or has reasonable cause to suspect that a child has suffered or faces a threat of suffering abuse or neglect.

Persons Responsible for the Child

Citation: Rev. Stat. §§ 2151.03(A); 2151.011

Responsible persons include:

- The child's parents, guardian, or custodian
- Other persons responsible for the child's care

Exceptions

Citation: Rev. Stat. §§ 2151.03(B); 2151.031; 2919.22

Nothing in this chapter shall be construed as subjecting a parent to criminal liability when, solely in the practice of religious beliefs, the parent fails to provide adequate medical or surgical care or treatment for the child. This section:

- Does not abrogate or limit any person's responsibility to report child abuse or neglect that is known or reasonably suspected or believed to have occurred, and to report children who are known to face or are reasonably suspected or believed to be facing a threat of suffering abuse or neglect

- Does not preclude any exercise of the authority of the State, any political subdivision, or any court to ensure that medical or surgical care or treatment is provided to a child when the child's health requires it

A child exhibiting evidence of corporal punishment or other physical disciplinary measure by a parent is not an abused child if the measure is not prohibited under § 2919.22 [that prohibits cruel or excessive means of discipline].

Oklahoma

Physical Abuse

Citation: Ann. Stat. Tit. 10A, § 1-1-105

Abuse means harm, threatened harm, or failure to protect from harm or threatened harm, to the health, safety, or welfare of a child by a person responsible for the child's health, safety, or welfare, including, but not limited to, nonaccidental physical or mental injury, sexual abuse, or sexual exploitation.

Harm or threatened harm to the health or safety of a child means any real or threatened physical, mental, or emotional injury or damage to the body or mind that is not accidental, including, but not limited to, sexual abuse, sexual exploitation, neglect, or dependency.

Heinous and shocking abuse includes, but is not limited to, aggravated physical abuse that results in serious bodily, mental, or emotional injury. *Serious bodily injury* means injury that involves:

- A substantial risk of death
- Extreme physical pain
- Protracted disfigurement
- A loss or impairment of the function of a body member, organ, or mental faculty
- An injury to an internal or external organ or the body
- A bone fracture
- Sexual abuse or sexual exploitation
- Chronic abuse, including, but not limited to, physical, emotional, or sexual abuse, or sexual exploitation that is repeated or continuing

- Torture, including, but not limited to, inflicting, participating in, or assisting in inflicting, intense physical or emotional pain upon a child repeatedly over a period of time for the purpose of coercing or terrorizing a child for the purpose of satisfying the craven, cruel, or prurient desires of the perpetrator or another person
- Any other similar aggravated circumstance

Neglect

Citation: Ann. Stat. Tit. 10A, § 1-1-105

Neglect means any of the following:

- The failure of omission to provide any of the following:
    - Adequate nurturance and affection, food, clothing, shelter, sanitation, hygiene, or appropriate education
    - Medical, dental, or behavioral health care
    - Supervision or appropriate caregivers
    - Special care made necessary by the physical or mental condition of the child
- The failure or omission to protect a child from exposure to any of the following:
    - The use, possession, sale, or manufacture of illegal drugs
    - Illegal activities
    - Sexual acts or materials that are not age-appropriate
- Abandonment

Heinous and shocking neglect includes, but is not limited to:

- Chronic neglect, including a persistent pattern of family functioning, in which the caregiver has not met or sustained the basic needs of a child that results in harm to the child
- Neglect that has resulted in a diagnosis for the child of failure to thrive
- An act or failure to act by a parent that results in the death or near death of a child or sibling, serious physical or emotional harm; sexual abuse or sexual exploitation; or presents an imminent risk of serious harm to a child
- Any other similar aggravating circumstance

Sexual Abuse/Exploitation

Citation: Ann. Stat. Tit. 10A, § 1-1-105

Harm or threatened harm to a child's health or safety includes, but is not limited to, sexual abuse or sexual exploitation.

Sexual abuse includes, but is not limited to, rape, incest, and lewd or indecent acts or proposals made to a child, as defined by law, by a person responsible for the child's health, safety, or welfare.

Sexual exploitation includes, but is not limited to:

- Allowing, permitting, or encouraging a child to engage in prostitution, as defined by law, by a person responsible for the child's health, safety, or welfare
- Allowing, permitting, encouraging, or engaging in the lewd, obscene, or pornographic photographing, filming, or depicting of a child in those acts by a person responsible for the child's health, safety, or welfare

Emotional Abuse

Citation: Ann. Stat. Tit. 10A, § 1-1-105

Harm or threatened harm to a child's health or safety includes, but is not limited to, mental injury.

Abandonment

Citation: Ann. Stat. Tit. 10A, § 1-1-105

Abandonment means:

- The willful intent by words, actions, or omissions not to return for a child
- The failure to maintain a significant parental relationship with a child through visitation or communication in which incidental or token visits or communication are not considered significant
- The failure to respond to notice of deprived proceedings

Standards for Reporting

Citation: Ann. Stat. Tit. 10A, § 1-2-1 01

A report is required when a person has reason to believe that a child is a victim of abuse or neglect.

Persons Responsible for the Child

Citation: Ann. Stat. Tit. 10A, § 1-1-105

Person responsible for a child's health, safety, or welfare includes:

- A parent, legal guardian, custodian, or foster parent
- A person age 18 or older with whom the child's parent cohabits or any other adult residing in the home of the child
- An agent or employee of a public or private residential home, institution, facility, or day treatment program or an owner, operator, or employee of a child care facility

Exceptions

Citation: Ann. Stat. Tit. 10A, § 1-1-105

Nothing contained in this act shall prohibit any parent, teacher, or other person from using ordinary force as a means of discipline, including, but not limited to, spanking, switching, or paddling.

A child is not considered abused or neglected for the sole reason that the parent, in good faith, selects and depends upon spiritual means alone through prayer, in accordance with the tenets and practice of a recognized church or religious denomination, for the treatment or cure of disease or remedial care of such child. Nothing contained in this paragraph shall prevent a court from immediately assuming custody of a child and ordering whatever action may be necessary, including medical treatment, to protect the child's health or welfare.

No medical treatment of a child with a disability shall be necessary if, in the reasonable medical judgment of the attending physician, such treatment would be futile in saving the life of the child.

Oregon

Physical Abuse

Citation: Rev. Stat. § 419B.005

Abuse means:

- An assault on a child and physical injury to a child that has been caused by other than accidental means, including injury that appears to be at variance with the explanation given of the injury
- Threatened harm to a child, that means subjecting a child to a substantial risk of harm to the child's health or welfare
- Permitting a person under age 18 to enter or remain in or upon premises where methamphetamine is being manufactured
- Unlawful exposure to a controlled substance that subjects a child to a substantial risk of harm to his or her health or safety

Neglect

Citation: Rev. Stat. § 419B.005

The term *abuse* includes negligent treatment or maltreatment of a child, including but not limited to, the failure to provide adequate food, clothing, shelter, or medical care that is likely to endanger the health or welfare of the child.

Sexual Abuse/Exploitation

Citation: Rev. Stat. § 419B.005

The term *abuse* includes:

- Rape of a child, which includes but is not limited to, rape, sodomy, unlawful sexual penetration, and incest
- Sexual abuse as described in chapter 163
- Sexual exploitation, including, but not limited to:
  - Contributing to the sexual delinquency of a minor
  - Conduct that allows, employs, authorizes, permits, induces, or encourages a child to engage in the performing for people to observe, or the photographing, filming, tape recording, or other

exhibition that, in whole or in part, depicts sexual conduct or contact, sexual abuse involving a child, or rape of a child
- Allowing, permitting, encouraging, or hiring a child to engage in prostitution

Emotional Abuse

Citation: Rev. Stat. § 419B.005

The term *abuse* includes any mental injury to a child that shall include only observable and substantial impairment of the child's mental or psychological ability to function caused by cruelty to the child, with due regard to the culture of the child.

Abandonment

This issue is not addressed in the statutes reviewed.

Standards for Reporting

Citation: Rev. Stat. § 419B.010

A report is required when there is reasonable cause to believe that a child has suffered abuse.

Persons Responsible for the Child

Citation: Rev. Stat. § 419B.005

Responsible person may include any person.

Exceptions

Citation: Rev. Stat. § 419B.005

Abuse does not include reasonable exercise of parental discipline.

Pennsylvania

Physical Abuse

Citation: Cons. Stat. Tit. 23, § 6303

Child abuse means any of the following:

- Any recent act or failure to act by a perpetrator that causes nonaccidental serious physical injury to a child under age 18
- Any recent act, failure to act, or series of such acts or failures to act by a perpetrator that creates an imminent risk of serious physical injury to a child under age 18

Serious bodily injury means bodily injury that creates a substantial risk of death or causes serious permanent disfigurement or protracted loss or impairment of function of any bodily member or organ.

Serious physical injury means an injury that causes a child severe pain or significantly impairs a child's physical functioning, either temporarily or permanently.

Nonaccidental means an injury that is the result of an intentional act that is committed with disregard of a substantial and unjustifiable risk.

Neglect

Citation: Cons. Stat. Tit. 23, § 6303

The term *child abuse* includes serious physical neglect by a perpetrator constituting prolonged or repeated lack of supervision or the failure to provide essentials of life, including adequate medical care, that endangers a child's life or development or impairs the child's functioning.

Sexual Abuse/Exploitation

Citation: Cons. Stat. Tit. 23, § 6303

The term *child abuse* means any of the following:

- An act or failure to act by a perpetrator that causes sexual abuse or sexual exploitation of a child under age 18

- Any recent act, failure to act, or series of such acts or failures to act by a perpetrator that creates an imminent risk of sexual abuse or sexual exploitation of a child under age 18

Sexual abuse or exploitation means any of the following:

- The employment, use, persuasion, inducement, enticement, or coercion of a child to engage in, or assist another individual to engage in, sexually explicit conduct
- The employment, use, persuasion, inducement, enticement, or coercion of a child to engage in, or assist another individual to engage in, simulation of sexually explicit conduct for the purpose of producing a visual depiction, including photographing, videotaping, computer depicting, and filming
- Any of the following offenses committed against a child:
    - Rape
    - Sexual assault
    - Involuntary deviate sexual intercourse
    - Aggravated indecent assault
    - Molestation
    - Incest
    - Indecent exposure
    - Prostitution
    - Sexual abuse
    - Sexual exploitation

Emotional Abuse

Citation: Cons. Stat. Tit. 23, § 6303

The term *child abuse* includes an act or failure to act by a perpetrator that causes nonaccidental serious mental injury to a child under age 18.

Serious mental injury means a psychological condition, as diagnosed by a physician or licensed psychologist, including the refusal of appropriate treatment, that:

- Renders a child chronically and severely anxious, agitated, depressed, socially withdrawn, psychotic, or in reasonable fear that his or her life or safety is threatened

- Seriously interferes with a child's ability to accomplish age-appropriate development and social tasks

Abandonment

This issue is not addressed in the statutes reviewed.

Standards for Reporting

Citation: Cons. Stat. Tit. 23, § 6311

A report is required when there is reasonable cause to suspect that a child is a victim of abuse.

Persons Responsible for the Child

Citation: Cons. Stat. Tit. 23, § 6303

A perpetrator is a person who has committed child abuse and is:

- A parent of a child
- A person responsible for the welfare of a child
- An individual residing in the same home as a child
- A paramour of a child's parent

Person responsible for the child's welfare means a person who provides permanent or temporary care, supervision, mental health diagnosis or treatment, training, or control of a child in lieu of parental care, supervision, and control. The term does not include a person who is employed by or provides services or programs in a public or private school, intermediate unit, or area vocational-technical school.

Exceptions

Citation: Cons. Stat. Tit. 23, § 6303

No child shall be deemed to be physically or mentally abused based on injuries that result solely from environmental factors that are beyond the control of the parent or person responsible for the child's welfare, such as inadequate housing, furnishings, income, clothing, and medical care.

If, upon investigation, the county agency determines that a child has not been provided needed medical or surgical care because of seriously held religious beliefs of the child's parents, and such beliefs are consistent with those of a *bona fide* religion, the child shall not be deemed to be physically or mentally abused. The county agency shall closely monitor the child and shall seek court-ordered medical intervention when the lack of medical or surgical care threatens the child's life or long-term health.

In cases involving religious circumstances, all correspondence with a subject of the report and the records of the Department of Public Welfare and the county agency shall not reference 'child abuse' and shall acknowledge the religious basis for the child's condition, and the family shall be referred for general protective services, if appropriate.

Puerto Rico

Physical Abuse

Citation: Ann. Laws Tit. 8, § 444

Abuse means any intentional act or omission by the father, mother, or other person in charge of the minor of such a nature that it causes or puts a minor at risk of suffering damage or harm to his or her health or physical, mental, and/or emotional integrity, including sexual abuse. Abuse shall also mean:

- Allowing another person to cause or to put the minor at risk of suffering damage or harm to his or her health or physical, mental, and/or emotional integrity
- Willfully abandoning a minor
- Allowing the father, mother, or other person in charge of the well-being of the minor to exploit him or her
- Allowing another person to exploit the minor by forcing or allowing the minor to perform any act, including but not limited to obscene acts for profit or in order to receive any other benefit, or to incur in any conduct that, if criminally prosecuted, would constitute a crime against the health or physical, mental, or emotional integrity of the minor, including sexual abuse of the minor

Minors will also be considered to be victims of abuse if the father, mother, or person responsible for the minor has engaged in acts that constitute domestic violence in the presence of minors.

Physical harm means any nonaccidental trauma, injury, or condition, including inadequate nourishment that, if left unattended, could result in death, disfigurement, illness, or temporary or permanent disability of any part or function of the body, including inadequate nourishment. The trauma, injury, or condition may also be the result of a single episode or several episodes.

Neglect

Citation: Ann. Laws Tit. 8, § 444; Tit. 31, § 634a(3)

Neglect means a type of abuse that consists of failing to perform the duties or to exercise the capacity to provide adequate food, clothing, shelter, education, or health care to a minor; failing to exercise supervision; or failing to visit the minor or to remain in contact or frequent communication with the minor.

It is also considered neglect when the parent fails to comply with the duties or exercise the powers provided in title 31, § 601(1). These duties include, but are not limited to, the duty of having the minor in his or her company according to law, of supervising his or her education and development, of adequately providing sustenance, clothing, shelter, education or health care, according to his or her wealth or with the means provided by the Commonwealth or any natural or juridical person. Health care includes any treatment or preventive measure required to attend to or prevent any condition involving the physical, mental, or emotional health of the minor.

Sexual Abuse/Exploitation

Citation: Ann. Laws Tit. 8, § 444

The term *abuse* also means to engage in obscene behavior and/or use the minor to carry out obscene acts.

Sexual abuse means engaging in sexual conduct in the presence of a minor and/or using the minor, voluntarily or otherwise, to engage in sexual conduct aimed at satisfying lasciviousness, or any other act that, if criminally prosecuted, would constitute the crime of rape, sodomy, lewd or lascivious acts, indecent exposure, or obscene propositioning; or remitting, transporting, selling, distributing, publishing, exhibiting, or possessing obscene materials and obscene shows.

Emotional Abuse

Citation: Ann. Laws Tit. 8, § 444

Mental or emotional harm means the impairment of the intellectual or emotional capacity of a minor, given what is considered normal for his or her age or cultural environment. Moreover, emotional harm is deemed to exist when there is evidence that the minor recurrently manifests or exhibits behaviors such as fear, feelings of abandonment or hopelessness, frustration and failure, anxiety, insecurity, withdrawal, regressive behavior, or aggressive behavior toward himself or herself or toward others, or any other similar behavior.

Abandonment

Citation: Ann. Laws Tit. 8, § 444

Abandonment means willful dereliction of or being remiss in the responsibilities that the father, mother, or other person in charge of the minor have, taking into account the minor's age and need for adult care. The intention to abandon can be evidenced by, but is not limited to:

- A lack of communication with the minor for a period of at least 3 months
- A lack of participation in a plan or program designed to reunite the minor with the father, mother, or other person in charge of the well-being of the minor
- A failure to respond to notices of hearings for protection of the minor
- When the minor is found in circumstances that make it impossible to ascertain the identity of the father or mother; when the identity is known, but the whereabouts of the person is unknown, in spite of effort to locate him or her; or when the father or mother fails to claim the minor within 30 days after the minor is found

Standards for Reporting

Citation: Ann. Laws Tit. 8, § 446

A report is required when a person learns or comes to suspect that a minor has been or is at risk of becoming a victim of abuse or neglect.

Persons Responsible for the Child

Citation: Ann. Laws Tit. 8, § 444

Responsible persons include the minor's father, mother, or person responsible for the welfare of the minor.

Exceptions

Citation: Ann. Laws Tit. 31, § 634a(3)

No person may be deprived of *patria potestas* for the legitimate practice of his or her religious beliefs. However, when due to the above, the person fails to provide the minor with specifically prescribed health care, the court shall provide adequate remedies to attend to the health of the minor, and in appropriate cases, shall deprive the person of his or her *de jure* or *de facto* guardianship, or even of *patria potestas* as may be best for the minor's health.

Rhode Island

Physical Abuse

Citation: Gen. Laws § 40-11-2

Abused and/or neglected child means a child whose physical or mental health or welfare is harmed or threatened with harm when his or her parent or other person responsible for his or her welfare:

- Inflicts or allows to be inflicted upon the child physical or mental injury, including excessive corporal punishment
- Creates or allows to be created a substantial risk of physical or mental injury to the child, including excessive corporal punishment

Shaken baby syndrome means a form of abusive head trauma characterized by a constellation of symptoms caused by other than accidental traumatic injury resulting from the violent shaking and/or impact upon an infant or young child's head.

Neglect

Citation: Gen. Laws § 40-11-2

The term *abused and/or neglected child* includes a child whose physical or mental health or welfare is harmed or threatened with harm when the child's parent or other person responsible for his or her welfare:

- Fails to supply the child with adequate food, clothing, shelter, or medical care, although financially able to do so or offered financial or other reasonable means to do so
- Fails to provide the child with a minimum degree of care or proper supervision or guardianship because of his or her unwillingness or inability to do so by situations or conditions such as, but not limited to, social problems, mental incompetency, or the use of a drug, drugs, or alcohol to the extent that the parent or other person responsible for the child's welfare loses his or her ability or is unwilling to properly care for the child

Sexual Abuse/Exploitation

Citation: Gen. Laws § 40-11-2

The term *abused and/or neglected child* includes a child whose physical or mental health or welfare is harmed or threatened with harm when his or her parent or other person responsible for his or her welfare:

- Commits or allows to be committed against the child an act of sexual abuse
- Sexually exploits the child in that the person allows, permits, or encourages the child to engage in prostitution
- Sexually exploits the child in that the person allows, permits, encourages, or engages in the obscene or pornographic photographing, filming, or depiction of the child in a setting that, taken as a whole, suggests to the average person that the child is about to engage in or has engaged in any sexual act, or that depicts any such child under age 18 performing sodomy, oral copulation, sexual intercourse, masturbation, or bestiality
- Commits or allows to be committed any sexual offense against the child

- Commits or allows to be committed against any child an act involving sexual penetration or sexual contact if the child is under age 15; or if the child is age 15 or older, and (1) force or coercion is used by the perpetrator or (2) the perpetrator knows or has reason to know that the victim is a severely impaired person or physically helpless

Emotional Abuse

Citation: Gen. Laws § 40-11-2

Mental injury includes a state of substantially diminished psychological or intellectual functioning related to, but not limited to, such factors as failure to thrive, ability to think or reason, control of aggressive or self-destructive impulses, acting-out or misbehavior, that include incorrigibility, ungovernability, or habitual truancy. The injury must be clearly attributable to the unwillingness or inability of the parent or other person responsible for the child's welfare to exercise a minimum degree of care toward the child.

Abandonment

Citation: Gen. Laws § 40-11-2

The term *abused and/or neglected child* includes a child whose physical or mental health or welfare is harmed or threatened with harm when his or her parent or other person responsible for his or her welfare abandons or deserts the child.

Standards for Reporting

Citation: Gen. Laws § 40-11-3

A report is required when there is reasonable cause to know or suspect that a child has been abused or neglected.

Persons Responsible for the Child

Citation: Gen. Laws § 40-11-2

Person responsible for child's welfare means:

- The child's parent or guardian
- Any individual, age 18 age or older, who resides in the home of a parent or guardian and has unsupervised access to a child

- A foster parent
- An employee of a public or private residential home or facility
- Any staff person providing out-of-home care

Exceptions

No exceptions are specified in statute.

South Carolina

Physical Abuse

Citation: Ann. Code § 63-7-20

Child abuse or neglect or *harm* occurs when the parent, guardian, or other person responsible for the child's welfare:

- Inflicts or allows to be inflicted upon the child physical or mental injury or engages in acts or omissions that present a substantial risk of physical or mental injury to the child, including injuries sustained as a result of excessive corporal punishment
- Abandons the child
- Encourages, condones, or approves the commission of delinquent acts by the child and the commission of the acts are shown to be the result of the encouragement or approval
- Has committed abuse or neglect as described above such that a child who subsequently becomes part of the person's household is at substantial risk of one of those forms of abuse or neglect

Physical injury means death or permanent or temporary disfigurement or impairment of any bodily organ or function.

Neglect

Citation: Ann. Code § 63-7-20

Child abuse or neglect or *harm* occurs when the parent, guardian, or other person responsible for the child's welfare fails to supply the child with adequate food, clothing, shelter, education as required by law; supervision appropriate to the child's age and development; or health care even though financially able to do so or offered financial or other reasonable means to do so and the failure to do so has caused or presents a substantial risk of causing physical or mental injury.

Sexual Abuse/Exploitation

Citation: Ann. Code § 63-7-20

Child abuse or neglect or *harm* occurs when the parent, guardian, or other person responsible for the child's welfare commits or allows to be committed against the child a sexual offense as defined by the laws of this State or engages in acts or omissions that present a substantial risk that a sexual offense as defined in the laws of this State would be committed against the child.

Emotional Abuse

Citation: Ann. Code § 63-7-20

Mental injury means an injury to the intellectual, emotional, or psychological capacity or functioning of a child as evidenced by a discernible and substantial impairment of the child's ability to function when the existence of that impairment is supported by the opinion of a mental health professional or medical professional.

Abandonment

Citation: Ann. Code § 63-7-20

Abandonment of a child means a parent or guardian willfully deserts a child or willfully surrenders physical possession of a child without making adequate arrangements for the child's needs or the continuing care of the child.

Standards for Reporting

Citation: Ann. Code § 63-7-310

A report is required when there is reason to believe that a child has been abused or neglected.

Persons Responsible for the Child

Citation: Ann. Code § 63-7-20

Person responsible for a child's welfare includes:

- The child's parent, guardian, or foster parent
- An operator, employee, or caregiver, as defined by § 63-13-20, of a public or private residential home, institution, agency, or child care facility
- An adult who has assumed the role or responsibility of a parent or guardian for the child, but who does not necessarily have legal custody of the child

A person whose only role is as a caregiver and whose contact is only incidental with a child, such as a babysitter or a person who has only incidental contact but may not be a caregiver, has not assumed the role or responsibility of a parent or guardian.

Exceptions

Citation: Ann. Code § 63-7-20

The term child abuse or neglect excludes corporal punishment or physical discipline that:

- Is administered by a parent or person *in loco parentis*
- Is perpetrated for the sole purpose of restraining or correcting the child
- Is reasonable in manner and moderate in degree
- Has not brought about permanent or lasting damage to the child
- Is not reckless or grossly negligent behavior by the parents

A child's absences from school may not be considered abuse or neglect unless the school has made efforts to bring about the child's attendance, and those efforts were unsuccessful because of the parents' refusal to cooperate.

South Dakota

Physical Abuse

Citation: Ann. Laws § 26-8A-2

Abused or neglected child means a child:

- Whose parent, guardian, or custodian has subjected the child to mistreatment or abuse
- Who was subject to prenatal exposure to abusive use of alcohol, marijuana, any controlled drug, or a substance not lawfully prescribed by a practitioner

Neglect

Citation: Ann. Laws § 26-8A-2

The term *abused or neglected child* includes a child:

- Who lacks proper parental care through the actions or omissions of the child's parent, guardian, or custodian
- Whose environment is injurious to the child's welfare
- Whose parent, guardian, or custodian fails or refuses to provide proper or necessary subsistence, supervision, education, medical care, or any other care necessary for the child's health, guidance, or well-being
- Who is homeless, without proper care, or not domiciled with the child's parent, guardian, or custodian through no fault of the child's parent, guardian, or custodian
- Whose parent, guardian, or custodian knowingly exposes the child to an environment that is being used for the manufacture, use, or distribution of methamphetamine or any other unlawfully manufactured controlled drug or substance

Sexual Abuse/Exploitation

Citation: Ann. Laws § 26-8A-2

The term *abused or neglected child* includes a child who is subject to sexual abuse, sexual molestation, or sexual exploitation by the child's parent, guardian, custodian, or any other person responsible for the child's care.

Emotional Abuse

Citation: Ann. Laws § 26-8A-2

The term *abused or neglected child* includes a child who has sustained emotional harm or mental injury as indicated by an injury to the child's intellectual or psychological capacity, evidenced by an observable and substantial impairment in the child's ability to function within the child's normal range of performance and behavior, with due regard to the child's culture.

Abandonment

Citation: Ann. Laws § 26-8A-2

The term *abused or neglected child* includes a child whose parent, guardian, or custodian has abandoned the child.

Standards for Reporting

Citation: Ann. Laws § 26-8A-3

A report is required when there is reasonable cause to suspect that a child has been abused or neglected.

Persons Responsible for the Child

Citation: Ann. Laws § 26-8A-2

Responsible persons include a child's parent, guardian, or custodian.

Exceptions

No exceptions are specified in statute.

Tennessee

Physical Abuse

Citation: Ann. Code § 37-1-102

Abuse exists when a person under age 18 is suffering from, has sustained, or may be in immediate danger of suffering from or sustaining a wound, injury, disability, or physical or mental condition caused by brutality, neglect, or other actions or inactions of a parent, relative, guardian, or caregiver.

Severe child abuse means:

- The knowing exposure of a child to or the knowing failure to protect a child from abuse or neglect that is likely to cause great bodily harm or death, and the knowing use of force on a child that is likely to cause great bodily harm
- Specific brutality, abuse, or neglect toward a child that in the opinion of qualified experts has caused or will reasonably be expected to produce severe psychosis, severe neurotic disorder, severe depression, severe developmental delay or retardation, or severe impairment of the child's ability to function adequately in the child's environment, and the knowing failure to protect a child from such conduct
- The knowing failure to protect the child from the commission of any such act toward the child
- Knowingly allowing a child to be present within a structure where the act of creating methamphetamine is occurring

Neglect

Citation: Ann. Code § 37-1-102

Dependent and neglected child means a child:

- Who is without a parent, guardian, or legal custodian
- Whose parent, by reason of cruelty, mental incapacity, immorality, or depravity is unfit to care properly for the child
- Who is under unlawful or improper care, supervision, custody, or restraint by any person, corporation, agency, association, institution, society, or other organization or who is unlawfully kept out of school

- Whose parent or guardian neglects or refuses to provide necessary medical, surgical, institutional, or hospital care
- Who, because of lack of proper supervision, is found in a place the existence of which is in violation of law
- Who is in a condition of such want or suffering, or is under such improper guardianship or control, as to injure or endanger his or her morals or health
- Who is suffering from abuse or neglect
- Who has been in the care and control of one or more agencies or persons not related by blood or marriage for a continuous period of 6 months or longer in the absence of a power of attorney or court order, and that person or agency has not initiated judicial proceedings seeking either legal custody or adoption of the child
- Who is or has been allowed, encouraged, or permitted to engage in prostitution or obscene or pornographic photographing, filming, posing, or similar activity, and whose parent or guardian neglects or refuses to protect the child from further such activity
- Who willfully has been left in the sole financial and physical care of a related caregiver for not less than 18 consecutive months by the child's parent(s) or legal custodian, and the child will suffer substantial harm if removed from the continuous care of such relative

Sexual Abuse/Exploitation

Citation: Ann. Code § 37-1 -602

Child sexual abuse means the commission of any act involving the unlawful sexual abuse, molestation, fondling, or carnal knowledge of a child under age 13 that, on or after November 1, 1989, constituted the criminal offense of:

- Aggravated rape, sexual battery, or sexual exploitation of a minor
- Criminal attempt for any of the offenses listed above
- Especially aggravated sexual exploitation of a minor
- Incest
- Rape, sexual battery, or sexual exploitation of a minor

Child sexual abuse also means one or more of the following acts:

- Any penetration, however slight, of the vagina or anal opening of one person by the penis of another person, whether or not there is the emission of semen
- Any contact between the genitals or anal opening of one person and the mouth or tongue of another person
- Any intrusion by one person into the genitals or anal opening of another person, including the use of any object for this purpose
- Intentional touching of the genitals or intimate parts, including the breasts, genital area, groin, inner thighs, and buttocks, or the clothing covering them, of either the child or the perpetrator
- Intentional exposure of the perpetrator's genitals in the presence of a child, or any other sexual act intentionally perpetrated in the presence of a child, if such exposure or sexual act is for the purpose of sexual arousal or gratification, aggression, degradation, or other similar purpose
- Sexual exploitation of a child, which includes allowing, encouraging, or forcing a child to solicit for or engage in prostitution or engage in sexual exploitation

Emotional Abuse

Citation: Ann. Code § 37-1 -602

Mental injury means an injury to the intellectual or psychological capacity of a child as evidenced by a discernible and substantial impairment in the child's ability to function within the child's normal range of performance and behavior, with due regard to the child's culture.

Abandonment

This issue is not addressed in the statutes reviewed.

Standards for Reporting

Citation: Ann. Code §§ 37-1 -493; 37-1 -605

A report is required when a person knows or has reasonable cause to suspect that a child has been abused, neglected, or sexually abused.

Persons Responsible for the Child

Citation: Ann. Code §§ 37-1-102; 37-1 -602

Responsible persons include:

- The child's parent or guardian
- A person with whom the child lives
- Any *other person responsible for a child's care or welfare* that includes, but is not limited to:
    - A legal custodian or foster parent
    - An employee of a public or private child care agency or public or private school
    - Any other person legally responsible for the child's welfare in a residential setting

Exceptions

Citation: Ann. Code § 37-1 -602

Child sexual abuse does not include acts intended for a valid medical purpose or acts that may reasonably be construed to be normal caregiver responsibilities or interactions with or affection for a child.

Texas

Physical Abuse

Citation: Fam. Code § 261.001

Abuse means the following acts or omissions by a person:

- Physical injury that results in substantial harm to the child or the genuine threat of substantial harm from physical injury to the child, including an injury that is at variance with the history or explanation given and excluding an accident or reasonable discipline by a parent, guardian, or conservator that does not expose the child to a substantial risk of harm
- Failure to make a reasonable effort to prevent an action by another person that results in physical injury or substantial harm to the child

- The current use by a person of a controlled substance in a manner or to the extent that the use results in physical, mental, or emotional injury to a child
- Causing, expressly permitting, or encouraging a child to use a controlled substance

Neglect

Citation: Fam. Code § 261.001

Neglect means the following acts or omissions by a person:

- Placing a child in, or failing to remove a child from, a situation that a reasonable person would realize requires judgment or actions beyond the child's level of maturity, physical condition, or mental abilities and that results in bodily injury or a substantial risk of immediate harm to the child
- Failing to seek, obtain, or follow through with medical care for a child, with the failure resulting in or presenting a substantial risk of death, disfigurement, or bodily injury, or with the failure resulting in an observable and material impairment to the growth, development, or functioning of the child
- Failing to provide a child with food, clothing, or shelter necessary to sustain the life or health of the child, excluding failure caused primarily by financial inability unless relief services had been offered and refused
- Placing a child in, or failing to remove the child from, a situation in which the child would be exposed to a substantial risk of sexual conduct harmful to the child
- Placing a child in, or failing to remove the child from, a situation in which the child would be exposed to acts or omissions that constitute sexual abuse
- The failure by the person responsible for a child's care, custody, or welfare to permit the child to return to the child's home without arranging for the necessary care for the child after the child has been absent from the home for any reason, including having been in residential placement or having run away

Sexual Abuse/Exploitation

Citation: Fam. Code § 261.001

The term *abuse* includes the following acts or omissions by a person:

- Sexual conduct harmful to a child's mental, emotional, or physical welfare, including conduct that constitutes the offense of indecency with a child, sexual assault, or aggravated sexual assault
- Failure to make a reasonable effort to prevent sexual conduct harmful to a child
- Compelling or encouraging a child to engage in sexual conduct
- Causing, permitting, encouraging, engaging in, or allowing the photographing, filming, or depicting of a child if the person knew or should have known that the resulting photograph, film, or depiction of the child is obscene or pornographic
- Causing, permitting, encouraging, engaging in, or allowing a sexual performance by a child

Emotional Abuse

Citation: Fam. Code § 261.001

The term *abuse* includes the following acts or omissions by a person:

- Mental or emotional injury to a child that results in an observable and material impairment in the child's growth, development, or psychological functioning
- Causing or permitting a child to be in a situation in which the child sustains a mental or emotional injury that results in an observable and material impairment in the child's growth, development, or psychological functioning

Abandonment

Citation: Fam. Code § 261.001

The term *neglect* includes the leaving of a child in a situation where the child would be exposed to a substantial risk of physical or mental harm, without arranging for necessary care for the child, and the demonstration of intent not to return by a parent, guardian, or conservator of the child.

Standards for Reporting

Citation: Fam. Code § 261.101

A report is required when there is cause to believe that the child's physical or mental health has been adversely affected by abuse or neglect.

Persons Responsible for the Child

Citation: Fam. Code § 261.001

Person responsible for a child's care, custody, or welfare means a person who traditionally is responsible for a child's care, custody, or welfare, including:

- A parent, guardian, conservator, or foster parent of the child
- A member of the child's family or household, meaning persons living together in the same dwelling, without regard to whether they are related to each other, and includes persons who previously lived in the household
- A person with whom the child's parent cohabits
- School personnel or a volunteer at the child's school
- Personnel or a volunteer at a public or private child care facility that provides services for the child or at a public or private residential institution or facility where the child resides

Exceptions

Citation: Fam. Code § 261.001

Abuse does not include reasonable discipline by a parent that does not expose the child to substantial risk of harm.

Utah

Physical Abuse

Citation: Ann. Code § 78A-6-105

Abuse means:

- Nonaccidental harm of a child
- Threatened harm of a child

- Sexual exploitation or sexual abuse

Abused child means a child who has been subjected to abuse.

Physical abuse means abuse that results in physical injury or damage to a child.

Severe abuse means abuse that causes or threatens to cause serious harm to a child.

Neglect

Citation: Ann. Code § 78A-6-105

Neglect means:

- Lack of proper parental care of a child by reason of the fault or habits of the parent, guardian, or custodian
- Failure or refusal of a parent, guardian, or custodian to provide proper or necessary subsistence, education, or medical care, or any other care necessary for the child's health, safety, morals, or well-being
- A child at risk of being neglected or abused because another child in the same home is neglected or abused

Neglected child means a child who has been subjected to neglect.

Severe neglect means neglect that causes or threatens to cause serious harm to a child.

Sexual Abuse/Exploitation

Citation: Ann. Code § 78A-6-105

Sexual abuse means:

- An act or attempted act of sexual intercourse, sodomy, incest, or molestation directed toward a child
- Engaging in any conduct with a child that would constitute an offense under any of the following terms, regardless of whether the person who engages in the conduct is actually charged with, or convicted of, the offense:
    - Any sexual offense
    - Child bigamy
    - Incest

  - Lewdness or sexual battery
  - Lewdness involving a child
  - Voyeurism

Sexual exploitation means knowingly:

- Employing, using, persuading, inducing, enticing, or coercing any child to:
  - Pose in the nude for the purpose of sexual arousal of any person
  - Engage in any sexual or simulated sexual conduct for the purpose of photographing, filming, recording, or displaying in any way the sexual or simulated sexual conduct
- Displaying, distributing, possessing for the purpose of distribution, or selling material depicting a child:
  - In the nude, for the purpose of sexual arousal of any person
  - Engaging in sexual or simulated sexual conduct
- Engaging in conduct that would constitute an offense under Title 76, Chapter 5a, Sexual Exploitation of Children, regardless of whether the person who engages in the conduct is actually charged with, or convicted of, the offense

Incest means engaging in sexual intercourse with a person whom the perpetrator knows to be his or her ancestor, descendant, brother, sister, uncle, aunt, nephew, niece, or first cousin. This includes relationships of:

- The whole or half blood, without regard to legitimacy
- Parent and child by adoption
- Stepparent and stepchild while the marriage creating the relationship exists

Emotional Abuse

Citation: Ann. Code § 78A-6-105

Harm means physical, emotional, or developmental injury or damage.

Abandonment

Citation: Ann. Code § 78A-6-105

The term *neglect* includes abandonment of a child, except as provided in Title 62A, Chapter 4a, Part 8, Safe Relinquishment of a Newborn Child.

Standards for Reporting

Citation: Ann. Code § 62A-4a-403

A report is required when there is reasonable cause to believe that a child has been subjected to abuse or neglect.

Persons Responsible for the Child

Citation: Ann. Code § 62A-4a-402

A person responsible for a child's care means the child's parent, guardian, or other person responsible for the child's care, whether in the same home as the child; a relative's home; a group, family, or center daycare facility; a foster care home; or a residential institution.

Exceptions

Citation: Ann. Code § 78A-6-105

Abuse does not include:

- Reasonable discipline or management of a child, including withholding privileges
- The use of reasonable and necessary physical restraint or force on a child in self-defense, in defense of others, to protect the child, or to remove a weapon in the possession of a child in self-defense or defense of others

A parent or guardian legitimately practicing religious beliefs and who, for that reason, does not provide specified medical treatment for a child, is not guilty of neglect. A health-care decision made for a child by the child's parent or guardian does not constitute neglect unless the State or other party to the proceeding shows by clear and convincing evidence that the health-care decision is not reasonable and informed. Nothing in this subsection may prohibit a parent or guardian from exercising the right to obtain a second health-care opinion.

Vermont

Physical Abuse

Citation: Ann. Stat. Tit. 33, § 4912

Abused or neglected child means a child whose physical health, psychological growth and development, or welfare is harmed or is at substantial risk of harm by the acts or omissions of his or her parent or other person responsible for the child's welfare.

Harm can occur by physical injury.

Physical injury means death, permanent or temporary disfigurement, or impairment of any bodily organ or function by other than accidental means.

Neglect

Citation: Ann. Stat. Tit. 33, § 4912

Harm can occur by failure to supply the child with adequate food, clothing, shelter, or health care.

Sexual Abuse/Exploitation

Citation: Ann. Stat. Tit. 33, § 4912

The term *abused or neglected child* includes a child who is sexually abused or at substantial risk of sexual abuse by any person.

Sexual abuse consists of an act or acts by any person that involves sexual molestation or exploitation of a child including, but not limited to, incest, prostitution, rape, sodomy, or any lewd and lascivious conduct involving a child.

Sexual abuse also includes aiding, abetting, counseling, hiring, or procuring a child to perform or participate in any photograph, motion picture, exhibition, show, representation, or other presentation that, in whole or in part, depicts sexual conduct, sexual excitement, or sadomasochistic abuse involving a child.

Emotional Abuse

Citation: Ann. Stat. Tit. 33, § 4912

Harm can be caused by emotional maltreatment.

Emotional maltreatment means a pattern of malicious behavior that results in a child's impaired psychological growth and development.

Abandonment

Citation: Ann. Stat. Tit. 33, § 4912

Harm can be caused by the abandonment of the child.

Standards for Reporting

Citation: Ann. Stat. Tit. 33, § 4913

A report is required when there is reasonable cause to believe that a child has been abused or neglected.

Persons Responsible for the Child

Citation: Ann. Stat. Tit. 33, § 4912

A person responsible for a child's welfare includes:

- The child's parent, guardian, or foster parent
- Any other adult residing in the home who serves in a parental role
- An employee of a public or private residential home, institution, or agency
- Any other person responsible for the child's welfare while in a residential, educational, or child care setting, including any staff person

Exceptions

Citation: Ann. Stat. Tit. 33, § 4912

A parent or other person responsible for a child's care legitimately practicing his or her religious beliefs who thereby does not provide specified medical treatment for a child shall not be considered neglectful for that reason alone.

Virgin Islands

Physical Abuse

Citation: Ann. Code Tit. 5, § 2502

Abuse means any physical injury inflicted on a child, other than by accidental means, by those responsible for the care and maintenance of the child, which causes or creates substantial risk of death, serious or protracted disfigurement, protracted impairment of physical health, or loss or protracted impairment of the function of any bodily organ.

Imminent danger to that child's life or health means danger that involves:

- Substantial physical pain
- Serious bodily injury resulting in physical disfigurement
- Substantial impairment of the function of a bodily member or organ
- Injury that may result in death

Neglect

Citation: Ann. Code Tit. 5, § 2502

Neglect means the failure of those responsible for the care and maintenance of the child to provide the necessary support, maintenance, education, and medical or mental health care, to the extent that the child's health or welfare is harmed or threatened thereby.

Sexual Abuse/Exploitation

Citation: Ann. Code Tit. 5, § 2502

The term *abuse* includes the sexual abuse of a child, as defined by law, or the sexual exploitation of a child, including the prostituting of a child, and the photographing or other depiction of a child for pornographic purposes, or a persistent course of sexual conduct that causes a child's health or welfare to be harmed or threatened.

Imminent danger to that child's life or health means danger that involves actual or attempted sexual abuse.

Emotional Abuse

Citation: Ann. Code Tit. 5, § 2502

The term *abuse* includes any mental injury inflicted on a child that causes or creates substantial risk of impairment of emotional health.

Imminent danger to that child's life or health means danger that involves substantial impairment of the intellectual, psychological, or emotional capacity of a child caused by inhumane acts or conduct.

Abandonment

Citation: Ann. Code Tit. 5, § 2502

Abandoned child means a child whose parents, guardian, or custodian desert him or her for such a length of time and under such circumstances as to show an intent to evade the duty of rearing him or her or a reckless disregard for his or her needs.

- It shall be a rebuttable presumption that the parent intends to abandon the child who has been left without any provision for his or her support or without communication from such parent for a period of 6 months.
- If, in the opinion of the court, the evidence indicates that the parent has made only minimal efforts to support or communicate with the child, the court may declare the child to be abandoned.
- Abandonment is a form of neglect.

Standards for Reporting

Citation: Ann. Code Tit. 5, § 2533

A report is required when there is reasonable cause to suspect that a child has been subjected to abuse, sexual abuse, or neglect.

Persons Responsible for the Child

Citation: Ann. Code Tit. 5, § 2502

Person responsible for a child's care includes:

- The child's parent, guardian, or custodian

- A person or agency responsible for the child's welfare or care, whether the child is in his or her own home, shelter care, a detention home, a relative's home, a foster home, or a residential institution

Exceptions

No exceptions are specified in statute.

Virginia

Physical Abuse

Citation: Ann. Code § 63.2-100

Abused or neglected child means any child younger than age 18:

- Whose parents or other person responsible for his or her care creates or inflicts, threatens to create or inflict, or allows to be created or inflicted, upon the child a physical or mental injury by other than accidental means, or creates a substantial risk of death, disfigurement, or impairment of bodily or mental functions
- Who is with the parent or other responsible person either (1) during the manufacture or attempted manufacture of a schedule I or II controlled substance, or (2) during the unlawful sale of such substance, where such manufacture, or attempted manufacture or unlawful sale would constitute a felony violation
- Whose parents or other responsible person creates a substantial risk of physical or mental injury by knowingly leaving the child alone in the same dwelling, including an apartment, with a person to whom the child is not related by blood or marriage and who the parent or other responsible person knows has been convicted of an offense against a minor for which registration is required as a violent sexual offender

Neglect

Citation: Ann. Code § 63.2-100

Abused or neglected child means any child younger than age 18:

- Whose parents or other person responsible for his or her care neglects or refuses to provide care necessary for his or her health

- Who is without parental care or guardianship caused by the unreasonable absence or the mental or physical incapacity of the child's parent, guardian, legal custodian, or other person standing in loco parentis

Sexual Abuse/Exploitation

Citation: Ann. Code § 63.2-100

The term *abused or neglected child* includes any child younger than age 18 whose parents or other person responsible for his or her care commits or allows to be committed any act of sexual exploitation or any sexual act upon a child in violation of the law.

Emotional Abuse

Citation: Ann. Code § 63.2-100

The term *abused or neglected child* includes any child younger than age 18 whose parents or other person responsible for his or her care creates or inflicts, threatens to create or inflict, or allows to be created or inflicted upon the child a mental injury, or creates a substantial risk of impairment of mental functions.

Abandonment

Citation: Ann. Code § 63.2-100

The term *abused or neglected child* includes any child younger than age 18 whose parents or other person responsible for his or her care abandons the child.

Standards for Reporting

Citation: Ann. Code § 63.2-1509

A report is required when there is reason to suspect that a child is abused or neglected.

Persons Responsible for the Child

Citation: Ann. Code § 63.2-100

Responsible persons include the child's parents or another person responsible for the care of the child.

Exceptions

Citation: Ann. Code § 63.2-100

No child who in good faith is under treatment solely by spiritual means through prayer, in accordance with the tenets and practices of a recognized church or religious denomination, shall for that reason alone be considered to be an abused or neglected child. Further, a decision by parents who have legal authority for the child, or in the absence of parents with legal authority for the child, any person with legal authority for the child, who refuses a particular medical treatment for a child with a life-threatening condition shall not be deemed a refusal to provide necessary care if:

- The decision is made jointly by the parents or other person with legal authority and the child.
- The child has reached age 14 and is sufficiently mature to have an informed opinion on the subject of his or her medical treatment.
- The parents or other person with legal authority and the child have considered alternative treatment options.
- The parents, or other person with legal authority, and the child believe in good faith that such decision is in the child's best interests.

Washington

Physical Abuse

Citation: Rev. Code §§ 26.44.020; 26.44.030; 9A.1 6.100

Abuse or neglect means the injury of a child by any person under circumstances that cause harm to the child's health, welfare, or safety, or the negligent treatment or maltreatment of a child by a person responsible for or providing care to the child. An abused child is a child who has been subjected to child abuse or neglect.

Severe abuse means any of the following:

- Any single act of abuse that causes physical trauma of sufficient severity that, if left untreated, could cause death
- Any single act of sexual abuse that causes significant bleeding, deep bruising, or significant external or internal swelling
- More than one act of physical abuse, each of which causes bleeding, deep bruising, significant external or internal swelling, bone fracture, or unconsciousness

Any use of force on a child by any other person is unlawful unless it is reasonable and moderate and is authorized in advance by the child's parent or guardian for purposes of restraining or correcting the child. The following actions are presumed unreasonable when used to correct or restrain a child:

- Throwing, kicking, burning, or cutting a child
- Striking a child with a closed fist
- Shaking a child younger than age 3
- Interfering with a child's breathing
- Threatening a child with a deadly weapon
- Doing any other act that is likely to cause and that does cause bodily harm greater than transient pain or minor temporary marks

The age, size, and condition of the child and the location of the injury shall be considered when determining whether the bodily harm is reasonable or moderate. This list is illustrative of unreasonable actions and is not intended to be exclusive.

Neglect

Citation: Rev. Code §§ 26.44.020; 9A.42.100

Negligent treatment or maltreatment means an act or a failure to act, or the cumulative effects of a pattern of conduct, behavior, or inaction, that evidences a serious disregard of consequences of such magnitude as to constitute a clear and present danger to a child's health, welfare, or safety, including but not limited to conduct prohibited under § 9A.42.100 [endangerment with a controlled substance]. When considering whether a clear and present danger exists, evidence of a parent's substance abuse as a contributing factor to negligent treatment or maltreatment shall be given great weight.

It is *endangerment with a controlled substance* if the person knowingly or intentionally permits a dependent child to be exposed to, ingest, inhale, or have contact with methamphetamine or ephedrine, pseudoephedrine, or anhydrous ammonia, including their salts, isomers, and salts of isomers, that are being used in the manufacture of methamphetamine, including its salts, isomers, and salts of isomers.

Sexual Abuse/Exploitation

Citation: Rev. Code § 26.44.020

The term *abuse or neglect* includes the sexual abuse or sexual exploitation of a child by any person under circumstances that indicate that the child's health, welfare, and safety are harmed.

Sexual exploitation includes:

- Allowing, permitting, or encouraging a child to engage in prostitution by any person
- Allowing, permitting, encouraging, or engaging in the obscene or pornographic photographing, filming, or depicting of a child by any person

Emotional Abuse

This issue is not addressed in the statutes reviewed.

Abandonment

This issue is not addressed in the statutes reviewed.

Standards for Reporting

Citation: Rev. Code § 26.44.030

A report is required when there is reasonable cause to believe that a child has suffered abuse or neglect.

Persons Responsible for the Child

Citation: Rev. Code § 26.44.020

Any person can be a responsible person.

Exceptions

Citation: Rev. Code §§ 26.44.015; 26.44.020; 9A.16.100

This chapter shall not be construed to authorize interference with child-raising practices, including reasonable parental discipline, that are not injurious to a child's health, welfare, and safety.

Nothing in this chapter may be used to prohibit the reasonable use of corporal punishment as a means of discipline.

No parent or guardian may be deemed abusive or neglectful solely by reason of the parent's or child's blindness, deafness, developmental disability, or other handicap.

The fact that siblings share a bedroom is not, in and of itself, negligent treatment or maltreatment. Poverty, homelessness, or exposure to domestic violence that is perpetrated against someone other than the child does not constitute negligent treatment or maltreatment in and of itself.

A person who is being furnished Christian Science treatment by a duly accredited Christian Science practitioner will not be considered, for that reason alone, a neglected person.

The physical discipline of a child is not unlawful when it is reasonable and moderate and is inflicted by a parent, teacher, or guardian for purposes of restraining or correcting the child.

West Virginia

Physical Abuse

Citation: Ann. Code § 49-1-3

Abused child means a child whose health or welfare is harmed or threatened by:

- A parent, guardian, or custodian who knowingly or intentionally inflicts, attempts to inflict, or knowingly allows another person to inflict, physical injury or mental or emotional injury, upon the child or another child in the home

- Sexual abuse or sexual exploitation
- The sale or attempted sale of a child by a parent, guardian, or custodian in violation of the law
- Domestic violence, as defined by § 48-27-202
- Physical injury as a result of excessive corporal punishment

Child abuse and neglect or *child abuse or neglect* means physical injury of a child by a parent, guardian, or custodian who is responsible for the child's welfare under circumstances that harm or threaten the health and welfare of the child.

Imminent danger to the physical well-being of the child means an emergency situation in which the welfare or the life of the child is threatened. Such emergency situations may include:

- Nonaccidental trauma inflicted by a parent, guardian, custodian, sibling, or a babysitter or other caregiver
- A combination of physical and other signs indicating a pattern of abuse that may be medically diagnosed as battered child syndrome
- Sale or attempted sale of the child by the parent, guardian, or custodian

Serious physical abuse means bodily injury that creates a substantial risk of death or causes serious or prolonged disfigurement, prolonged impairment of health, or prolonged loss or impairment of the function of any bodily organ.

Neglect

Citation: Ann. Code § 49-1-3

Neglected child means a child:

- Whose physical or mental health is harmed or threatened by a present refusal, failure, or inability of the child's parent, guardian, or custodian to supply the child with necessary food, clothing, shelter, supervision, medical care, or education

- Who is presently without necessary food, clothing, shelter, medical care, education, or supervision because of the disappearance or absence of the child's parent or custodian

Child abuse and neglect or *child abuse or neglect* means negligent treatment or maltreatment of a child by a parent, guardian, or custodian who is responsible for the child's welfare under circumstances that harm or threaten the health and welfare of the child.

Imminent danger to the physical well-being of the child means an emergency situation in which the welfare or the life of the child is threatened. Such emergency situations may include:

- Nutritional deprivation
- Inadequate treatment of serious illness or disease

Sexual Abuse/Exploitation

Citation: Ann. Code § 49-1-3

Sexual abuse means:

- Engaging in, attempting to engage in, or knowingly procuring another person to engage in sexual intercourse, sexual intrusion, or sexual contact with a child younger than age 16, notwithstanding the fact that the child may have willingly participated in such conduct or the fact that the child may have suffered no apparent physical injury or mental or emotional injury as a result of such conduct
- Engaging in, attempting to engage in, or knowingly procuring another person to engage in sexual intercourse, sexual intrusion, or sexual contact with an child age 16 or older, notwithstanding the fact that the child may have consented to such conduct or the fact that the child may have suffered no apparent physical injury or mental or emotional injury as a result of such conduct
- Any conduct whereby a parent, guardian, or custodian displays his or her sex organs to a child or procures another person to display his or her sex organs to a child for the purpose of gratifying the sexual desire of the parent, guardian, or custodian, of the person making such display, or of the child, or for the purpose of affronting or alarming the child

Sexual exploitation means an act whereby a parent, guardian, or custodian:

- Whether for financial gain or not, persuades, induces, entices, or coerces a child to engage in sexually explicit conduct
- Persuades, induces, entices, or coerces a child to display his or her sex organs for the sexual gratification of the parent, guardian, custodian, or a third person, or to display his or her sex organs under circumstances in which the parent, guardian, or custodian knows such display is likely to be observed by others who would be affronted or alarmed

Emotional Abuse

Citation: Ann. Code § 49-1-3

The terms *child abuse and neglect* or *child abuse or neglect* include mental or emotional injury of a child by a parent, guardian, or custodian who is responsible for the child's welfare, under circumstances that harm or threaten the health and welfare of the child.

Imminent danger to the physical well-being of the child includes substantial emotional injury inflicted by a parent, guardian, or custodian.

Abandonment

Citation: Ann. Code § 49-1-3

Imminent danger to the physical well-being of the child includes abandonment by the parent, guardian, or custodian.

Standards for Reporting

Citation: Ann. Code § 49-6A-2

A report is required when there is reasonable cause to suspect that a child is neglected or abused.

Persons Responsible for the Child

Citation: Ann. Code § 49-1-3

Responsible persons include the child's parent, guardian, or custodian.

Exceptions

Citation: Ann. Code § 49-1-3

A child is not considered neglected when:

- The lack of necessary food, clothing, shelter, or medical care is due primarily to a lack of financial means on the part of the parent.
- The child's education is conducted within the provisions of § 18-8-1 [that provides exemption from State compulsory education requirement for private school enrollment or homeschooling].

Wisconsin

Physical Abuse

Citation: Ann. Stat. § 48.02

Abuse means any of the following:

- Physical injury inflicted on a child by other than accidental means
- When used in referring to an unborn child, serious physical harm inflicted on the unborn child, and the risk of serious physical harm to the child when born, caused by a habitual lack of self-control of the expectant mother of the unborn child in the use of alcohol beverages, controlled substances, or controlled substance analogs, exhibited to a severe degree
- Manufacturing methamphetamine in violation of § 961 .41(1)(e) under any of the following circumstances:
    - With a child physically present during the manufacture
    - In a child's home, on the premises of a child's home, or in a motor vehicle located on the premises of a child's home
    - Under any circumstances in which a reasonable person should have known that the manufacture would be seen, smelled, or heard by a child

Physical injury includes, but is not limited to, lacerations, fractured bones, burns, internal injuries, severe or frequent bruising, or great bodily harm.

Neglect

Citation: Ann. Stat. § 48.981

Neglect means failure, refusal, or inability of a parent, guardian, legal custodian, or other person exercising temporary or permanent control over a child, for reasons other than poverty, to provide necessary care, food, clothing, medical or dental care, or shelter so as to seriously endanger the physical health of the child.

Sexual Abuse/Exploitation

Citation: Ann. Stat. § 48.02

The term *abuse* includes any of the following:

- Sexual intercourse or sexual contact
- Sexual exploitation of a child
- Permitting, allowing, or encouraging a child to engage in prostitution
- Causing a child to view or listen to sexual activity
- The exposure of one's genitals to a child

Emotional Abuse

Citation: Ann. Stat. § 48.02

The term *abuse* includes emotional damage for which the child's parent, guardian, or legal custodian has neglected, refused, or been unable for reasons other than poverty to obtain the necessary treatment or to take steps to ameliorate the symptoms.

Emotional damage means harm to a child's psychological or intellectual functioning. Emotional damage shall be evidenced by one or more of the following characteristics exhibited to a severe degree: anxiety, depression, withdrawal, outward aggressive behavior, or a substantial and observable change in behavior, emotional response, or cognition that is not within the normal range for the child's age and stage of development.

Abandonment

This issue is not addressed in the statutes reviewed.

Standards for Reporting

Citation: Ann. Stat. § 48.981

A report is required when there is reasonable cause to suspect that a child has been abused or neglected.

Persons Responsible for the Child

Citation: Ann. Stat. § 48.981

Responsible persons include:

- The child's parent, guardian, or legal custodian
- Any other person exercising temporary or permanent control over a child

Exceptions

Citation: Ann. Stat. § 48.981

It is not considered neglect when the failure to provide a child with necessary care, food, clothing, shelter, medical, or dental care is due to poverty.

Wyoming

Physical Abuse

Citation: Ann. Stat. § 14-3-202

Abuse means inflicting or causing physical injury, harm, or imminent danger to the physical health or welfare of a child other than by accidental means, including excessive or unreasonable corporal punishment.

Physical injury means any harm to a child, including but not limited to disfigurement, impairment of any bodily organ, skin bruising if greater in magnitude than minor bruising associated with reasonable corporal punishment, bleeding, burns, fracture of any bone, subdural hematoma, or substantial malnutrition.

Neglect

Citation: Ann. Stat. § 14-3-202

The term *abuse* includes malnutrition or substantial risk of harm by reason of intentional or unintentional neglect.

Neglect means a failure or refusal by those responsible for the child's welfare to provide adequate care, maintenance, supervision, education, or medical, surgical, or any other care necessary for the child's well-being.

Sexual Abuse/Exploitation

Citation: Ann. Stat. § 14-3-202

The term *abuse* includes the commission or allowing the commission of a sexual offense against a child, as defined by law.

Emotional Abuse

Citation: Ann. Stat. § 14-3-202

The term *abuse* includes inflicting or causing mental injury or harm to the mental health or welfare of the child.

Mental injury means an injury to the psychological capacity or emotional stability of a child as evidenced by an observable or substantial impairment in his or her ability to function within a normal range of performance and behavior with due regard to his or her culture.

Abandonment

Citation: Ann. Stat. § 14-3-202

The term *abuse* includes abandonment, unless the abandonment is a relinquishment substantially in accordance with §§ 14-11-101 through 14-11-109.

Standards for Reporting

Citation: Ann. Stat. § 14-3-205

A report is required when a person knows or has reasonable cause to suspect that a child has been abused or neglected.

Persons Responsible for the Child

Citation: Ann. Stat. § 14-3-202

A person responsible for a child's welfare includes:

- The child's parent, noncustodial parent, guardian, custodian, stepparent, or foster parent
- Any other person, institution, or agency having the physical custody or control of the child

Exceptions

Citation: Ann. Stat. § 14-3-202

Treatment given in good faith by spiritual means alone through prayer by a duly accredited practitioner, in accordance with the tenets and practices of a recognized church or religious denomination, is not child neglect for that reason alone.

End Notes

[1] 42 U.S.C.A. § 5106g(2) (2003).

[2] 42 U.S.C.A. § 5106g(4) (2003).

[3] Massachusetts defines child abuse and neglect in regulation.

[4] The term "child" means a person who is younger than age 18. States also may define child abuse and neglect in their criminal statutes. These definitions provide the grounds for the arrest and prosecution of the offenders. For more information on the criminal aspects of child abuse and neglect, visit the National Center for Prosecution of Child Abuse website: www.ndaa.org/apri/programs/ncpca/statutes

[5] The word *approximately* is used to stress the fact that the States frequently amend their laws. This information is current through July 2009. The States are Alabama, Alaska, Arkansas, California, Colorado, Florida, Hawaii, Illinois, Indiana, Kansas, Kentucky, Louisiana, Maine, Maryland, Massachusetts, Michigan, Minnesota, Montana, Nebraska, Nevada, New Jersey, New Mexico, New York, North Carolina, Ohio, Oklahoma, Oregon, Pennsylvania, Rhode Island, South Carolina, Tennessee, Texas, Utah, Vermont, Virginia, West Virginia, Wisconsin, and Wyoming.

[6] The States that define "failure to educate" as neglect include Arkansas, Colorado, Connecticut, Delaware, Idaho, Indiana, Kentucky, Maine, Minnesota, Mississippi, Missouri, Montana, Nevada, New Hampshire, New Jersey, New Mexico, New York, North Dakota, Ohio, South Carolina, South Dakota, Utah, West Virginia, and Wyoming.

[7] Mississippi, North Dakota, Ohio, Oklahoma, Tennessee, Texas, and West Virginia.

[8] Indiana, Kansas, Minnesota, and Montana.

[9] All States except Georgia and Washington.

[10] Alaska, Arizona, Arkansas, California, Colorado, Delaware, Florida, Hawaii, Idaho, Iowa, Kansas, Kentucky, Maine, Maryland, Massachusetts, Minnesota, Montana, Nevada, New

Hampshire, New York, North Carolina, Ohio, Oregon, Pennsylvania, Rhode Island, South Carolina, South Dakota, Tennessee, Texas, Vermont, Wisconsin, and Wyoming.

[11] For summaries of statutes and a more complete discussion of this issue, see Child Welfare Information Gateway's *Parental Drug Use as Child Abuse:* www.childwelfare.gov/systemwide/laws_policies/statutes/dru gexposed.cfm

[12] Arizona, Arkansas, Colorado, Illinois, Indiana, Iowa, Louisiana, Massachusetts, Minnesota, North Dakota, Oklahoma, Oregon, South Dakota, and Wisconsin.

[13] Colorado, Indiana, Iowa, Montana, Ohio, Oregon, South Dakota, Tennessee, Virginia, and Washington.

[14] Arizona, Arkansas, and Washington.

[15] Arkansas, Florida, Hawaii, Illinois, Minnesota, Ohio, and Texas.

[16] California, Delaware, Kentucky, Minnesota, New York, Rhode Island, and Texas.

[17] California, Colorado, Connecticut, Illinois, Kentucky, Louisiana, Minnesota, Nevada, New Jersey, North Carolina, Rhode Island, South Dakota, Utah, Vermont, Virginia, West Virginia, and Wyoming.

[18] Arizona, Arkansas, Florida, Idaho, Indiana, Kansas, Maine, Massachusetts, Montana, Nebraska, New Hampshire, New Mexico, New York, North Dakota, Ohio, Oklahoma, South Carolina, and Texas.

[19] Arkansas, Florida, Kansas, Louisiana, Massachusetts, New Hampshire, North Dakota, Pennsylvania, Texas, Washington, West Virginia, and Wisconsin.

[20] Arkansas, California, Colorado, Florida, Georgia, Indiana, Minnesota, Mississippi, Missouri, Ohio, Oklahoma, Oregon, South Carolina, Texas, Utah, and Washington.

[21] Alabama, Alaska, California, Colorado, Delaware, Florida, Georgia, Idaho, Illinois, Indiana, Iowa. Kansas, Kentucky, Louisiana, Maine, Michigan, Minnesota, Mississippi, Missouri, Montana, Nevada, New Hampshire, New Jersey, New Mexico, Ohio, Oklahoma, Pennsylvania, Utah, Vermont, Virginia, and Wyoming.

[22] Alabama, Colorado, Florida, Idaho, Indiana, Iowa, Kansas, Kentucky, Louisiana, Michigan, Missouri, Montana, Nevada, Ohio, Oklahoma, and Pennsylvania.

[23] Arizona, Connecticut, and Washington.

[24] Michigan, Minnesota, Missouri, Ohio, and Oklahoma.

INDEX

F

G

H

I

J

K

L

M

N

O

P

Q

R

S